FROM

PRISON

TO PULPIT

One Man's True Story

of God's Life-Changing Power

Lawrence Oji

EVANGELISTA MEDIA™ srl
Via Maiella, 1
66020 San Giovanni Teatino (Ch)—Italy

"Changing the World, One Book at a Time"

This book and all other Evangelista Media™ and Destiny Image™ Europe books are available at Christian bookstores and distributors worldwide.

To order products, or for any other correspondence:

EVANGELISTA MEDIA™ srl
Via Maiella, 1
66020 San Giovanni Teatino (Ch)—Italy
Tel. +39 085 959806 • Fax: +39 085 9090113
Email: info@evangelistamedia.com

www.evangelistamedia.com

ISBN 13: 978-88-97896-96-8
ISBN 13 EBOOK: 978-88-97896-97-5

For Worldwide Distribution, Printed in Italy
3 4 5 6 7/ 18 17 16 15

This is a true story.
In certain cases, names of individuals
and details of their circumstances
have been changed or omitted
to protect their anonymity.

DEDICATION

I dedicate this book to you, my mother, Chief (Mrs.) Virginia Nnennaya Oji. Lolo, how can I forget all the sorrow, agony, and heartbreak I caused you for over twenty years?

When you attended my "passing out parade" at the Police College, Enugu, Nigeria, where I was awarded the "baton of honor" (Best Student Award), you watched the State Commissioner of Police hand over that prestigious award to me with pride and the hope that I would one day head the Nigerian Police Force.

I can now imagine the pain you went through when, just a few years later, these hopes were dashed. Through my actions, you became a subject of ridicule; you were openly mocked and taunted by "friends" and foes.

Though it looked as if I was destined to remain a junkie, a drug addict for life, you stood by me, always hoping and praying that God would one day turn my life around. I thank God that you also had my brother Francis, who kept telling you that I was not going to die in that world of darkness. Oh, how right he was!

Mother, today, those mockers have been forever silenced. God has indeed restored your joy just as you always believed.

He has turned your mourning into dancing. I pray that you will live long enough to indeed "recover all." Even though my father did not live long enough to see the beautiful children the Lord has blessed my marriage with, I pray that He will keep you long enough to see my children's children.

Mother, you've suffered shame for my sake. I pray you live long to enjoy fame for my sake too.

ACKNOWLEDGMENTS

First and foremost, I want to thank God Almighty for giving me a message for an entire life. *From Prison to Pulpit* is a lifetime message, and I will share this testimony for as long as I live.

My profound gratitude to you, sir, Rev. Dr. Paul Jinadu, General Overseer, New Covenant Church, for giving me the platform to express my calling, and for taking the time to write the endorsement for my book.

I thank you, sir, Pastor Dr. Tony Rapu, for writing the foreword to my book.

I wish to say a massive thanks to you, my Pastor, Reverend Tayo Arowojolu for recognizing the moment you heard my story that such deliverance can only be the work of God. What most people would have used to relegate me to the background, you understood as something to be used to demonstrate God's awesome power in transforming lives, and you did not hesitate to give me your support when I shared with you my vision to start SHADE (Saving Hands for Alcoholic and Drug End-Users). The acronym was, as usual, coined by you.

To my very special brother, Mario Lambri—words cannot express how much I appreciate you. Thank you for your financial support toward the publication of this book.

Special thanks to you, Pastor Nick Chima Okoro, for not giving up on me like so many others. You continuously prayed for my salvation and sowed a seed in 1990 when you bought me that famous Bible I sold for a peanut just to have another fix of crack cocaine. Truly, just as the Bible says, "One plants, another waters, but God gives the increase" (see 1 Cor. 3:6 NKJV). My testimony is also your testimony.

Engr. Nnamdi Udo, you have been a wonderful brother and a friend indeed. Your compassionate nature is unmatched, and I pray that the Lord will remember you only for good in Jesus' name, amen.

My brother, Greg-Obong Oshotse, I owe you a lot. Your support is beyond description, and the fact that it was through our friendship that I met my heartthrob, Stella-Maris, means this world to me. I appreciate you dearly.

To Pastor (Mrs.) Nike Akinsulire, I say thank you so much. You are more than a sister. You made me realize that I will not have peace until I put this testimony in a book, and you didn't allow me to have that peace until this book was written.

To Anna Sowley, I say thank you for your contribution. You painstakingly edited this book with a sister's heart.

To Lizzy Mang of Mang and Co., Solicitors, I express my heartfelt appreciation, for you have been a sister and a genuine friend.

To Andrew Prescott of KCM Prison Ministry and Mrs. Iris Little of Kings Church Prison Ministry, Wales, I say thanks for your constant correspondence and support while I was in prison and for travelling all the way to London to attend my ordination as a pastor. And to you, Lulawo Michael Olusegun, thanks for introducing me to Kenneth Copeland Prison Ministries.

I want to thank Evangelist Antonino Di Forte of Chiesa Sulla Roccia, Gela, Italy, for all his support to me while I was in prison in Caltanissetta and for giving me eighty Italian Bibles I used for evangelism the moment I left prison.

To my beautiful children—Sammy Okoyo, Favour Uchechi Abimbola, and Esther Ginikachim Nifemi—I thank you for always bringing me so much joy.

Finally, to you Stella-Maris, my own wifey, my Angel, my jewel of inestimable value, my Stainless, my secretary, this book would never have seen the light of day had I not met and married you. You worked tirelessly even when you were physically exhausted to ensure that I shared this testimony to God's glory. Thank you for believing in me. Thank you for loving me. Thank you for marrying me. You are indeed everything a man like me who had wasted years, could find and say without doubt, "Our God is truly a Restorer of lost years." You are indeed a star! Keep shining!

ENDORSEMENTS

Lawrence Oji is a man transformed by the grace of God, and now he is on a mission to lead others into all the fullness of what he himself has received. You will be blessed, inspired, and motivated as you read his amazing story in this book *From Prison to Pulpit*.

Rev. (Dr.) Paul Jinadu
General Overseer, New Covenant Church

On a bright May Day in 2003, a man walked into my law firm in London and sought my legal advice on some issues. I felt the issues we discussed concerned our beliefs, more than they did the law. It was as if the man was aggressively trying to convert me, not seeking legal solutions. It felt as if Jesus' second coming was imminent. The urgency in his demeanor caused me to invite him to our church for a "dominion hour" service. He then made a declaration that has become part of our testimony; he said, "I will attend the service, and after, I would know if you are to be my pastor or just my lawyer!" I was astounded by the depth of this statement. After that service he said to me, "You are my pastor." I also became his lawyer, just as he has become my evangelist, my brother, and my friend, for close to ten years now.

Having read this book, it dawned on me why Pastor Lawrence Oji takes Christianity and the winning of souls to Christ as an urgent assignment. It became apparent why at times it seems as if he's flying before he runs, running before he walks, and walking before he crawls. This book demonstrates God's impartial love, His desire that all may be saved despite their past, and the essence of Romans 8:28–35. Indeed, God is great, and He is the Solution to all our challenges in life.

My desire is that everyone in Christ—and, most particularly, anyone who feels all hope is lost—should read this book. Indeed, Isaiah 1:18–19 is very true.

A remarkable book from a remarkable man.

Tayo Arowojolu
Senior Pastor
New Covenant Church, Edmonton
London, UK

It was through my role as Prison Minister for Kenneth Copeland Ministries Europe that I had the privilege of corresponding with and playing a small role in this powerful story of Lawrence Oji's life. My prayer is that as you read this book, it will fill your heart with hope and give you faith to know that, no matter how low you go in life, no matter how dark the road gets or how much despair you face, there is a God who cares enough to reach into the midst of your circumstances, lift you out, and set you in a place of victory through the power of Jesus Christ our Lord.

Andrew Prescott
Prison Minister
Kenneth Copeland Ministries Europe

TABLE OF CONTENTS

FOREWORD

It gives me great pleasure to write this foreword. Lawrence Oji's powerful story is that of one man who, like many others, resorted to substance abuse amongst other vices in an attempt to find a panacea for life's pressures. Beyond that, it is the story of the magnitude of transformation that comes from an encounter with the life-changing power of God.

From Prison to Pulpit will help others find their way out of addictions. It demonstrates in a vivid and captivating way that God's love reaches into the darkest pit to rescue us—the masterpiece of His creation. I believe this book will not only help young people see the dangers ahead and avoid the pitfalls; it will also help parents detect the warning signs of substance abuse and delinquency early. It will help each one of us see how vulnerable we can be if our lives are not rooted in Christ.

Lawrence Oji found his purpose, satisfaction, and self-worth in God. This book is a must-read, and when you start, you will not want to put it down.

Dr. Tony Rapu
Senior Pastor, This Present House Church
Lagos, Nigeria

FOREWORD

He's now called "Pastor Solution!" Twenty-three years ago, he was "Mr. Problem"! Everyone—parents, relatives, friends, and pastors—had all but given up on him. Why? He was hooked on every imaginable drug and had literally lost every right to decent company; he was broke and so hungry that he even sold a Bible given to him as a gift in 1990 just to have another fix of cocaine. By 2001, he had spent time in many prisons and ended up in a high-security jail in Italy, awaiting deportation to Nigeria.

Then suddenly, when all hope was lost, the unexpected happened! Jesus the Savior reached down into that cold Italian jail, picked up a man already judged as dead among the living, and transformed him into a vessel of honor. Suddenly, the man who not only fed on but peddled all sorts of drugs in the dark places of Lagos and Italy became a new creation, born of the Spirit of God, totally abandoning the life of drugs and now leading people away from drugs to Jesus.

When I met him in London in 2004, I saw a man literarily "dry cleaned," a sharp contrast to the unkempt drug addict who fourteen years earlier used to visit me in my office in Lagos wearing bathroom slippers to beg for money to feed his stomach and, of course, his drug appetite. On seeing me, his first words were, "Please forgive me; I sold that Bible you bought for me in 1990 to buy a fix of cocaine."

I could not help but shout, "What hath God wrought!" (Num. 23:23). My "theology" about how God would save a soul and who is "qualified" for ministry has undergone a drastic paradigm shift after seeing Lawrence passionately witness to prisoners, prostitutes, and drug addicts in the streets of London with outstanding conversions.

The story of Lawrence Oji, now "Pastor Solution," will remind us that God is ever willing and able to save anyone, no matter the depth of sin and depravity the person may have descended into. Again, I exclaim, "What hath God wrought!"

Nicholas Okoro
Coordinator, Hebrews Eleven Continuation Network
Lagos, Nigeria

THE TIPPING POINT

*"Insanity is doing the same thing,
over and over again, and expecting different results."*

The soccer game came to an instant halt. The mere sight of this particular prison warden was enough to stop you dead in your tracks. He had no neutrality about him. His presence meant one of two things: good or bad news. You were either being transferred to another prison or you were being released. Normally if anyone was due for release, then it would be quite natural to be joyful at his appearance. But, of course, if no one was due for release, his presence could only mean one thing: bad news!

As we had been playing soccer for quite a while, we were panting like dogs in a hunt, and it was a struggle to bring our heaving chests under control. We were already drenched in sweat, but now it poured freely as the blood pounded wildly in our hearts and anxiety took mastery of our thoughts.

In spite of ourselves, we mustered that involuntary sense of gallows humour that only prisoners can fully understand and began to playfully chant the two words that defined the warden: *Libertà! Trasferimento! Liberty! Transfer!* But our playfulness was only skin deep. Underneath we were a riot of emotions.

So whose turn was it now, we wondered? None of us was due for release. That much was certain. I had been in prison for just one year, and I had three more years to go before I was due for release. Also certain, it slowly dawned on us, was the fact that this warden wasn't a bringer of good news today. Someone was obviously been transferred—and that was a dreaded thing.

"Asprilla! Asprilla!" The warden shouted with his hand raised to beckon his ward, as he walked slowly towards us. Now the cat was out of the bag. Everyone knew Asprilla. He was the Columbian soccer player with the Italian Soccer Club Parma. That summer in 1998 he had been very much in the news for his prowess in the field and was very popular with the crowds. Far away in north Italy where we were trapped in prison in the city of Padua, we had carefully nicknamed ourselves after soccer stars according to how well we thought we resembled them in style, prowess, and gamesmanship.

"Asprilla, come with me," said the warden as he reached the crowd.

By now all eyes were on the culprit, the unfortunate one. As the warden stood before us, looking directly at his quarry, the crowd broke to let the prisoner through.

And I stepped out. Asprilla was my nickname. I walked with him to the matricula, the prison front office where wardens handled many administrative issues. It was the longest walk I'd ever undertaken, although it was a mere twenty yards from the field to the office. My mind was filled with questions. *What's going on? Why am I being transferred? Where am I being taken? Would it be solitary? Or would I be sharing cells? Would I be allowed any freedoms? Would I be allowed out to mix with other inmates and play games?* There was no end to the turmoil that was spreading in my soul.

"Solution Lawrence Oji, you are now being released."

I was startled. It was the same warden. I looked at him, consternation written all over my face. *Is this a sick joke?* I wondered.

"Solution Lawrence Oji, you are now being released," echoed another officer seated behind the huge sprawling worktop built from wall to wall as though to protect those behind it from prisoners who might become provoked or lose their minds as a result of bad news delivered to them from their portals.

I was still in a daze when a third official handed me a flimsy plastic bag. It contained all my valuables: just a few practical daily necessities. I mumbled some thanks and made for the door before they changed their minds.

"Solution, when next?" asked one of the two behind the sprawling worktop. He'd checked the records and knew I had been in and out of prison at least six times. And he knew I would be back in again. That much was also certain because, like reservists, drug addicts are always prisoners.

So I walked free into the city with my release papers tucked into my pocket, after spending just over a year in Padua jail, for drug dealing and possession. When I had recovered from the shock of my surprise release, I began to feel upbeat and elated. I called up friends, and they invited me to stay at their house. Quickly the news spread, and by the time I arrived there, quite a party had assembled to celebrate my freedom. We drank and smoked, and the house became crowded with well-wishers. Drugs were in plentiful supply, and later that evening we did speedballs, smoking a mix of heroin and crack cocaine. I was free and high.

I was sitting on the stairs smoking with a group of friends, when a loud hammering started. Voices were raised, but it was a loud party, so it was not until we heard the sound of a door being kicked in that we realized that this was a raid. The police swarmed in, shouting; there was screaming and violence as people resisted arrest. We had no time to react before policemen had located my group, and our incriminating stash. I still had my release papers in my pocket.

I was so high that I actually pleaded with the *polizia* to let me enjoy a few more hours of freedom, waving my release papers as if I expected them to give me some sort of preferential treatment. Of course I was led off the same as everyone else and charged once again with possession. My high did not last long. Within a few hours I was back in the *matricula* of Padua prison, facing the same guard, who still sat behind the enormous desk. His earlier joke, "When next?" did not seem funny anymore, and this time he did not make any remarks at all.

The guard just looked at me, rolled his eyes, and dismissed me with a motion of his hand. I was taken back to my old cell. They hadn't even had time to replace me. That day was my tipping point. I felt then, that unless something changed drastically in my life, I would always be a prisoner. I had lost count of the number of times I had been arrested. It happened so often that it had become routine.

This endless, unchanging cycle, was insanity.

Chapter One

SON GONE ASTRAY

Any story of mine has to start with my mother. Virginia Oji was the only surviving child of twelve, and she was not expected to live long. She was given the nickname "Abo-Agui," meaning "any day she wakes up will be counted." My grandfather, with whom she then lived, was keen to see her married early, afraid that she would follow in the wake of her siblings and die, leaving him with nobody to carry on the family line. When, to his immense surprise, she made it into her teens, he lost no time in marrying her to my father, a civil service officer with the colonial administration. My father worked for the Ministry of Agriculture and was the first in his family to forge a new life in northern Nigeria. This was the equivalent of modern Nigerians joining the Diaspora in America or Europe—enormously beneficial, economically and socially, both for them and their families back home. He supported his siblings and also found them jobs in the north. For a proud man like my grandfather, this was a prestigious union, and justified the morally dubious, effectively "forced" marriage of his child.

It was the early 1950s. They packed the fourteen-year-old Virginia onto a northbound train with her few belongings and a photograph of my father in her pocket. The marriage had been arranged by both sets of parents down in Arochukwu, in Abia State, but my father was then working in the northern town of Kaduna. It was an arduous three-day journey from the south. When Virginia Oji stepped off the train at Kaduna station, it was just as well that she had a photograph of her new husband because she would not have been able to tell Moses Oji Nwa Oji Kanu apart from any other man in the crowd. She had never met him before. My father stood on the platform, excitedly waving a picture of my mother. She had been told to look out for the man holding her photograph, as that was the man she was now married to. It seems bizarre that such an important meeting was not more carefully planned. I dread to think what would have happened if the photographs had passed into the wrong hands!

The newlyweds moved from Kaduna to the village of Samaru, near Zaria, and that is where I was born. They lived in government quarters in a two-bedroom house with its own bathroom and kitchen—quite luxurious by local standards. The other women in the compound used to make fun of my mother, saying that she was far too young to be married and pregnant. Just a little girl with a big stomach. My mother ignored them. She went on to have seven other children between 1958 and 1978, two girls and five boys. My parents moved between towns quite frequently with my father's job. He was well-liked by the white colonial government officials, and they often kept him on to work with them at their next post because of his industrious and hardworking nature. Before 1966, we lived all over northern and middle-belt Nigeria—in Zaria, Sokoto, Kaduna, Dawadawa, Kano, Jos, Bukuru, and Rijom. In keeping with tradition, the children were named after the town of their birth. All my sisters and brothers have different place names. Mine is Dan Samaru.

This nomadic lifestyle was fairly disruptive. I remember attending at least five different primary schools in as many years, which prevented me from making any proper friends or really settling down anywhere. The challenges of constantly moving house did not daunt my mother. With her intelligence, she had been singled out at school and offered a scholarship to the renowned Aggrey Memorial College in Arochukwu. At the time, her family had refused, wanting her instead to concentrate on making a good marriage, but her lack of formal education did not prevent her from becoming a shrewd businesswoman and, later on, after the war, a local politician. She started up her own grocery store and kept poultry in order to sell the eggs and meat from the birds. In every town we moved to, she joined the Staff Wives' Association, always taking pivotal roles such as chairperson or treasurer.

Because the union between my grandparents had only produced one daughter, my grandfather had decided to marry again (firmly against the wishes and principles of his first wife, who was a staunch Catholic, but in keeping with cultural norms) in order to have more children. It was widely believed that the deaths of the eleven children were my grandmother's fault, and my grandfather blamed her entirely. She was thought to have something wrong with her, perhaps a curse hung over her. This ignorant view, fuelled by a widespread belief in juju black magic, dismissed the effects of disease, food poisoning, dirty water, malaria, heat stroke, and other numerous contributors to the country's high infant mortality. Nigeria still has one of the highest rates in the world, and in many areas, women are illogically still held responsible.

My grandma, in protest against this outrageous act of bigamy, cut off all relations with her husband and moved to a new home in Awgu in Enugu State. She built a life for herself independent of my grandfather. He—and consequently his entire family—had been banned from the Catholic Church on the occasion of his second marriage, and my grandmother fought hard for the right to receive Holy Communion. She argued that my grandfather's sin should not be brought to bear on her, as she did not condone it. She remained a devout Catholic all her life and even went to Enugu during the Pope's visit to Nigeria in February 1982 in order to catch a glimpse of him. In spite of the huge crowds, she actually managed to get close enough to kiss his hand.

She was a midwife and ran her own maternity home for the village women in Awgu. She also set up a finishing school for girls, which taught domestic skills such as sewing, knitting, cooking, and home care. I remember her teaching us the catechism. She wanted all her daughter's children to be brought up Catholic. As was to be expected, she was very close to my mother, her only living child. When my mother fell pregnant with me, she somehow contrived to be there just before the birth. She had a midwife's sense of timing. It was extremely important to her that she be there to deliver her first grandchild.

There was only one problem—my father wanted me to be born in the government hospital as the regulation stipulated. The facility had been provided as a perk for the staff, and it was certainly the safest, cleanest place in town to have a baby. On the day of the birth, my father went to work as normal. He had been assured by my grandmother that the pains my mother was experiencing were absolutely normal and did not signify anything. My mother, inexperienced, did not know what to expect and trusted in the expertise of my grandmother. My father insisted that he be called to take my mother to the hospital the minute anything happened. With him safely out of the way, my grandmother barricaded the door of the house against the prying eyes of nosey neighbors, locked the door, and awaited the birth. She made my mother walk back and forth behind the house, moving her hips to speed the birth process. Before my mother realized what was happening she had gone into labor, and I was born in the bedroom of the house. My grandmother knew what she was doing, and everything went smoothly, but my father was quite furious when he found out he had been tricked! Ever since, the "official" story has been that I was born in Wusasa Hospital in Zaria, so that my father's employers and friends would not think that he had spurned the facilities offered to him.

My father named me after himself, as his firstborn son. I inherited the name that had been passed down from my paternal grandfather—Oji-Kanu. This became my middle name. My father had inherited this name as a special mark of respect and love from my grandfather. He was not the firstborn son of my grandfather, who had twenty wives and numerous children, but he nevertheless became the favorite son, singled out with this recognition. All his life he worked hard to bring honor to his father's name and to live up to the reputation he had been given. He was a stickler for excellence, and I looked up to him as a role model. He was overjoyed to have a son, and my uncle Emmanuel, who was working in my father's office at the time, beat the rhythm of an Ohafia war dance in celebration. Fast and powerful, this unique dance celebrates life and prosperity, the muscular drum language inspiring joy in all who hear it.

THE MAKING OF "LAWMAN BROWN" (1964)

My father was prosperous and highly commended for his hard work. Compared to other children living in our native town of Arochukwu, I had everything. The government quarters up north were comfortable. We had a sitting room and two bedrooms, our own kitchen and bathroom, situated in a well-planned compound with around fifteen other families in houses of identical design. I had a bicycle, which I rode around the compound, and a large red ball. This sticks in my memory because I was the only child to have these things to play with. Even compared to the children of other civil servants, I was privileged, let alone in comparison with children from my hometown. We didn't have a television of our own, but I remember watching an exciting boxing match—Cassius Clay (Muhammad Ali) versus Floyd Patterson—in the home of one of my father's white colleagues. My father was so well-liked that we were often invited over. I suppose you could say that we were treated differently from the majority of Nigerian civil servants.

My family sent me back to Arochukwu in 1964, along with my sister Catherine, to reconnect with our roots. I was the only child in town to have a bicycle, with the exception of the son of the famous Alvan Azinna Ikoku, which marked me out immediately as being in a privileged position. Dr. Ikoku had set up our local school, Aggrey Memorial College, back in 1932. It is a pleasant and spacious complex of low, white buildings, set around grassy squares, fringed with palm trees. A memorial to Dr. Ikoku now stands in its grounds. A bust of his head and shoulders, complete with black mortarboard and academic gown, watches over his grave and that of his most senior wife, Grace Goomsu. When I was at school, he was very much alive and politically active, bringing the same passion to politics that he did to his excellent teaching and school management. He championed the virtues of hard work and testified to the power of knowledge, which inspired all his students.

Aggrey Memorial College was where my mother would have gone to school, had her parents permitted it, and my sister and I attended Aggrey Primary School during my year at home. We lived in my paternal grandfather's compound, an entire village in itself comprising twenty huts for each of his twenty wives and concubines, surrounding a central "chief" house where my grandfather lived. This house had four rooms and was the biggest in the compound. The different wives would take it in turns to provide food for him each day. My grandfather would eat his meals in the company of all his children. He loved to be surrounded by his offspring. My extended family lived in the town itself, and I often stopped by to see my favorite uncle, who used to invite me to hang out with him after school.

This uncle loved me enormously, but to show his affection he would share with me his passion for marijuana. I was still a very young boy, but I would sit with him and his friends as they smoked weed, drank, and gambled, in what he used to call his "joint." It was well-known in town, and many big men, politicians and the like, used to come there. He had frequent run-ins with the police, but he always managed to bribe them to go away, and he carried on running his "joint" for many years. He nicknamed me "Lawman Brown," probably ironically, its meaning known only to him. My uncle used to roll his marijuana cigarettes in blue writing paper. While I sat with him, watching him roll them, he gave me a puff or two. The weed was so strong and potent that it sent me sky high, and I would go home afterward feeling extremely tired and hungry. My first experience was one I will never forget. The drug had a very powerful effect on such a small child, and I began to hallucinate. The ground rose from beneath me and came up toward my eyes. Spatially everything morphed and changed. I could not keep my balance, and I felt dizzy. But I loved the rush it gave me, and the feeling of floating away.

It quickly became a habit. I would stop by to see my uncle both before and after school, and he would give me one or two more puffs of marijuana. I don't think he had any idea that he was causing an addiction. To him, it was just a sign of affection. I began to fall asleep in class, my eyes red and my reactions dulled. I did not perform as well at school, and my teacher became very concerned as I had hitherto been a very bright and hardworking student. She got somebody to take me home one day because she thought I must have contracted an illness. Little did she know that her small pupil had a drug addiction.

I hid my secret well. My uncle never told anybody, and although I used to be at his house nearly every day in the company of men who used copious amounts of marijuana, nobody connected the two. I also took up smoking tobacco and took cigarettes with me for the journey to and from school, even picking up cigarette butts to smoke from the road and around the compound. My parents, of course, were not there to supervise me, remaining that year with the other children in the north, and they had no idea that I was anything but a model child and student.

At Christmas though, my parents returned to Arochukwu for the holidays, and everything came out. Whenever I wanted to smoke at home, I used to find an empty hut in the compound when one of my grandfather's wives was out visiting or shopping at the market. Round the back of the hut, where there was nothing but grass and trees, I would not be overlooked by any of the other dwellings and could indulge my habit undisturbed. One day near Christmas, I was smoking as usual behind one of the empty huts and was discovered by my mother who had come to look for me. The first thing she wanted to do on her arrival at Arochukwu was to find me and see how I was. She was horrified to find me hiding behind the hut with a cigarette in my mouth. Her immediate reaction was to smack the cigarette out of my mouth, leaving a burning sensation on my lips. She then burst into tears, asking me how I could do such a thing to her. I felt terribly ashamed and tremendously guilty, dreading to imagine how upset she would have been if she had known about the marijuana. This incident convinced her that I should not live apart from my parents anymore, as I was not receiving the correct upbringing. She never mentioned to me whether she had found out about my uncle's role in all of this. I suspect she must have known, really, because I never had much contact with him again. Little did I know at the time that I had become addicted to hard drugs; it would affect nearly forty years of my life.

Chapter Two

CIVIL WAR

The war came as a shock to everyone. Of course the political situation had been brewing for some time, but nobody expected outright war. The four years from 1966 to 1970 were a time of great heartache for people of Eastern Nigeria. Families were separated, many lost loved ones, and we children grew up very fast. I honestly think that by the end of that war, there were no children left in Nigeria. For me, and for many others involved in the fighting, it was natural to turn to drugs in order to gain some relief from the trauma. But even drugs could not erase the memories of what we had been witness to. I still remember everything vividly. The war also made me painfully aware of ethnic difference—I was Igbo or Nyamiri, and I was made to feel that I was different from other Nigerians. This was a matter of life and death to Igbos living in Northern Nigeria at that time. Almost overnight, Igbos were labeled as the "Enemy of the Nigerian People." Biafran.

My schooling in Riyom, where we had moved to by that time, was interrupted very abruptly. One day in 1966 I was told not to go to school anymore, but to stay home with my family. In the northern states it had begun to be very dangerous for anyone of Igbo extraction to go out in public. It is not for me to attempt a history of the war or to suggest the cause of it—the causes are still confused, and the reasons behind events remain unclear. However, a very brief introduction to the time is necessary. After the attempted coup by several Nigerian military leaders in January 1966, order was briefly restored by General Johnson Aguiyi-Ironsi. However, because he was an Igbo, people began to suspect him of an organized plot to take over the country and put the government into Igbo hands. He was killed in a countercoup a few months later when many Igbo army officers were also executed. After the coup, the violence began to be targeted more generally against civilians, specifically Igbo Christians living in the north. Months of extremist, hate-filled violence terrorized the population, and tens of thousands of Igbos were injured or killed when they were unable to escape in time. We moved to Bukuru in the middle belt in the hope that it would be safer for us, but ended up staying only a few months. The violence was spreading, even to the Plateau State.

A wholesale exodus began in order to escape the pogrom. My father went to work as usual one day, and in the sudden confusion of the arrival of the mobs, there was no time to contact him at the office. My mother and the five children—myself, Catherine, Samuel, Glory, and Christopher, who was only a baby—had to rush down to the station and try to get onto a train heading south. My father would later flee from his office, afraid for his life, but at the time we had no idea whether he was alive or dead. He never made it to the train station that day. We left with nothing; all our belongings we abandoned in fear, and all around us were a sea of refugees streaming toward the platform. The station was heaving with people desperately trying to get on the train. There were not enough cars, not enough room for everyone. The train cars were so packed that people began to crush and trample each other just to get on board. Some died of suffocation. There was such an air of panic and desperation that there was no consideration for others. People climbed onto the roofs of the cars, spilled out of the open doors, and clambered over each other in the scramble on the platform. Somehow my mother managed to get all five children inside a car. I remember the stifling heat of all those bodies packed together. People were crying; babies were screaming. We kept close to mother, but there was nothing she could do to make us comfortable. There was no room to sit down, and there was nowhere to go to the toilet. It was miserable enough for adults, let alone for small children.

The train stopped at Kafanchan as scheduled, but as soon as the engine pulled to a halt, an angry mob stormed the cars. They had been waiting for us, knowing the southbound train would be full of Igbo refugees. There was a police presence at the station, but the small number of officers could do nothing against such a crowd, and they were quickly overwhelmed. The mob was indiscriminate in its violence. There was no special treatment for women and children. There was nowhere for us to hide. Mother was powerless to protect us. She could not even protect herself. Everyone was in danger as hundreds of men forced their way through the carriages, shouting and wielding the most brutal weapons. I witnessed terrible acts of violence.

For some reason, nobody touched my family. We were all very lucky to be left alive, and we counted it as a miracle. We carried on down to Umuahia, which was the last stop on the line. The driver refused to stop again after Kafanchan to avoid any more scenes of carnage, and the train steamed straight through any other stations en route, leaving crowds of refugees behind. The jubilation of the people at Umuahia was such a contrast to the horror we had witnessed at Kafanchan. Families were reunited with loved ones, and those who had made it through were tearfully received back into their native homes. We still had to wait for our own father to arrive. We had not had any word from him, and this was a very anxious period for us all, especially my mother. Every day we would wonder when our turn for good news would come—and if it would ever come. We stayed with relatives for a couple of nights, and then journeyed by road to Arochukwu, back to my Father's native village. We had to wait months before we heard any news of my father, and when he did finally come to join us in Arochukwu, we also celebrated like the others.

SEX FOR SALT

My father worked for a while in Umuahia, and I went to an Anglican boarding school there. The rest of the family went back to Arochukwu, where my brother Francis was born. We also lost my brother Christopher, aged two, to dysentery. My time at boarding school only lasted about six months. By the summer, my father had taken me out of school and back to Arochukwu. Ever since the pogrom, we had been anticipating some sort of Igbo response, and it had come in May 1967, when Emeka Ojukwu declared the Eastern region to be the new Republic of Biafra. An Igbo army was created, headed by General Ojukwu. The war then officially began when Federal troops entered the Republic. My father got work at the Biafran Fuel Directorate, handing out rations of petrol. We also had an uncle (my father's immediate younger brother) who worked for the Food Directorate, so though the food supply to Igbo areas was patchy, we had enough to eat throughout the war. My father, to his credit, chose not to exploit his position and never sold fuel or supplies on the black market, even though it would have been very profitable to do so. He was scrupulously honest.

My mother, ever the savvy businesswoman, took advantage of the food scarcity to start trading in salt, which was not readily available. In fact, in 1967 many people had so little salt for cooking with that sodium deficiency became common. There was also widespread malnutrition because food imports were restricted by Federal blockades. A huge number of cases of *Kwashiorkor* (severe malnutrition) occurred in children caused by lack of nutrients, particularly protein. Federal troops destroyed a lot of farmland, and in many areas, people died of starvation. My mother used to journey to the war front in order to buy salt. The war fronts attracted markets because the Federal troops had access to supplies and foodstuffs which were not available in the south. She spoke Hausa, the northern language, as well as Ibo, and this allowed her to travel without attracting notice. However, it was still extremely dangerous, and she risked her life many times just to come back to Arochukwu with a sack of salt. This was worth a fortune in the south, and when she sold it, she made enough money to buy food for our entire family.

The village women coveted my mother's salt. Many could not afford to buy very much of it. Out of compassion for their situation, I stole small amounts to give them. Soon though, they began to exploit my kindness, asking me to steal larger amounts. I did not want my mother to find out that I had been stealing our family's livelihood, so I tried to avoid taking any more. To encourage me to keep the supply coming, the women soon started to offer me sexual favors in return for salt. They knew that I had no use for money. There was nothing to spend it on anyway, but it would look odd for a young boy to suddenly start flashing money around. I was only thirteen and was easily pressured into doing their bidding. When when I tried to stop, they threatened to tell my mother. Terrified she would find out about my bad behavior, I submitted to the blackmail and continued to steal salt. My first experiences of women, then, were with those who were willing to cheat and steal and manipulate. I was too young to understand the desperation these women were driven by, and my compassion for them quickly turned to contempt.

FIGHTING FOR BIAFRA

The following year I went with my father and younger brother Samuel to Uyo to receive Civil Defense Training. There was no press-ganging, no force needed. Everybody wanted to help the Igbo war effort—all who were able volunteered for military duty, including young boys—and it was considered honorable for me to go and train to become a soldier. The "Boy's Company" training camp in Uyo was full of boys like myself, and it was like something out of the adventure books. We were taught how to use a gun, how to clean and maintain it, how to fire it. We had target practice. We ran through the grass, taking cover, building defenses, and sneaking up on the "enemy" playacted by other boys. We spent long hours watching enemy positions, learning how to spy. After our training my father went back to Arochukwu to continue his work at the fuel directorate.

It was then that I became a boy soldier. I worked undercover for about a year. We dressed in rags, making ourselves look like orphans who had been left destitute by the death of our parents, and with this disguise, we hung around the Federal camps collecting information. The Federal soldiers used to take pity on us and take us in, feeding us and giving us shelter. After a few nights, we would then run away, back to the Biafran camp, and inform on the Federal troops. For a while this worked very well, and we were an invaluable resource, but eventually the Federal soldiers got wise. Once our cover had been blown, they started killing all the small boys they found near the Federal barracks, regardless of where they came from, just in case they were in the employ of the Biafran army.

My uncle Emmanuel Oji, who formerly worked on the railways in Zaria, was a major in the Biafran army. As soon as it became too dangerous for me to be a spy anymore, he recruited me to join his specialist squad stationed in Asaga-Ohafia called the Immortal Battalion. Top Biafran officers attended the launch of the Battalion, including Emeka Ojukwu himself. I was stationed with officers, providing support and personal assistance. Around the beginning of 1969, I became an orderly to one of the army officers stationed in Okigwe.

This was a wonderful job for a young boy, as I got all the special privileges associated with higher-ranking officials. I accompanied my officer everywhere in his private car, sitting in front with the driver in my nice uniform. Every time we arrived somewhere, I would open the car door for him, giving him a special salute, the "officer compliment." We were given good food, too. I felt important in my uniform. I aped the behavior of the officers, emulating my superiors. Going into the market, we could take whatever we liked without paying for it. Nobody would stop us because we were soldiers. As soon as they saw the uniform, people would comply with our orders. The people we protected were also scared of us. There was a lot of exploitation of women, too. The uniform was often used as an excuse for sexual crimes. We could have any woman we wanted, even if they were married. They were just put in the car and taken back to the barracks. Their husbands dared not object to the officers. Amongst the boy soldiers there was little sense of right and wrong. We just copied the others.

One day in May 1969, we were travelling in convoy along a road in enemy territory. Suddenly a grenade exploded behind one of the cars. One of the other orderlies that I knew was killed instantly, and several officers were wounded. I was lucky not to be hurt. My uncle heard about the incident and thought the area far too dangerous for me to be in. He looked out for me, and for the sake of my family did not want me to be in a situation where I could be killed. He took me on as his own personal orderly for a few months, to get me out of harm's way. Toward the end of the year we began to lose quite badly to the Federal Army. They gained more and more ground, and my uncle deemed it safer for me to go back to my family in Arochukwu. Philip Effiong, now General Chief of Staff, surrendered to the Federal Army on January 12, 1970, having taken charge of the Biafran cause after Ojukwu had fled to the Ivory Coast. We had essentially lost the war already. He saw that there was nothing to be gained from continuing to fight.

Aftermath

Directly after the war, Igbo property was seized all over the country. The government announced that all these houses were "abandoned property," even though in many cases the Igbos who had lived in them tried to return home. It was fortunate, then, that we didn't have our own property in the north, having lived in government quarters; nevertheless, we had lost everything when we had fled to the south. There were no more privileged jobs at the fuel or food directorate for my father or his relatives. We had to begin again.

I returned to school in April 1970. I had a brief spell at Aggrey Memorial College in Arochukwu, but then our family moved to Aba where my father had started a new job. In addition to studying, I worked both before and after school to help my mother in the market. We all had to sell what we could in order to make enough money to eat. In the mornings I would sell *akamu* (pap) and *akara* (bean cake). In the evening I would attempt to sell *okrika* (secondhand clothes). I had to run to market with my tray of wares, sell whatever I could, then run home, drop the tray, and try to catch up with my classmates on the four-mile-long stretch of road leading to the school. Most days I was late and was punished by the teacher, but as I had to help my mother, I just accepted the punishment as something I could not change. After school, I would run to meet my mother in the market where she would be waiting with some food and a change of clothes. I ate hurriedly and then took a bundle of clothes to carry round the city in search of customers. The money I made selling *okrika* was needed to augment the family income. My father no longer earned enough to support us all. When it began to get dark, I would come home for dinner and then go out to the junction on the high road to sell kerosene, eggs, and bread to the passing traffic. I would often stay out there past midnight until I had made enough money.

One particular evening I was out on the high road with my bundle of secondhand clothes, and a man on a bike approached me. He said he worked for Nigerian Breweries in Aba and wanted to buy lots of nice clothes for his wife. He told me that he lived about eight miles away and asked if I would bring the clothes to his house. He would pay me on arrival as it saved him carrying them there himself. I was overjoyed at the prospect of such a big sale and happily ran the eight miles alongside his bicycle. All the way there I imagined how proud my mother would be when I told her about the sale.

It took us about half an hour to reach a string of low huts. In the dark I could not see exactly where we were, but I made a note of their position on the road. He did not invite me into his house, but instead stood outside looking through the bundle of clothes. He picked out several of the best dresses, worth a good amount of money, and my eyes lit up. My family lived not too far away, so when he asked me if I had change for a banknote, I said I would run home and get it for him. I honestly felt that nothing would be too much trouble for this valuable customer. It had not been a good day for sales—in fact I had not made a single one—which made me even more keen to please. I was desperate not to go home empty-handed.

It did not take me more than twenty minutes to do the round-trip, and I ran back to the place I had left him with a handful of change I had gotten from my mother. I had left him looking through the rest of the bundle, saying that he would choose another dress, and I was expecting to find him waiting with his choices and ready to pay. Looking back, I cannot believe that I was so naïve. When I arrived outside the house, there was nobody there! The man had vanished, and with him had gone not only all the nice dresses, but also the entire selection of clothes. The bundle had been worth about three months wages to our family.

I stood for a few minutes in utter confusion, unable to believe that a grown man would steal from a child. I also wondered what I would tell my mother. My jubilation quickly turned to despair, as I knew she would be very upset. I walked all the way to the Nigerian Breweries, hoping to catch him there, or get some information as to his whereabouts. Of course he was not there, and nobody had ever heard of him. It suddenly occurred to me that I had no chance of finding him. He had never given me his name. From then on I was very careful not to trust anybody. I realized that some people would go to any length just to make a bit of money. The war had brought everybody low.

Chapter Three

PICKING UP THE PIECES

In spite of our financial troubles, my parents decided that I should return to proper education, and in the summer of 1970, I was sent to a boy's boarding school in Aba, called Ibo National High School. During the war, the building had been used as barracks for the Biafran troops (as indeed had most schools and public buildings), and later as accommodation for Federal soldiers, so the place no longer resembled much of a school. We had to make do without furniture, as it had all been burnt as firewood. There were no desks or chairs. We had concrete breezeblocks to sit on if we were lucky, and we balanced our notebooks on our knees to write down what the teacher said. I managed to learn despite the chaos of my surroundings, and luckily the teachers found that I had natural ability.

There was one girl in Ibo National High School. She was called Ugo. It was rather odd, considering it was an all-boy's school, and I never knew the reason why she came, but amongst three or four hundred male students, there she was. She walked among us like some sort of queen, set apart. You can imagine that every boy there wanted her to be his girlfriend. Admittedly, the odds were against me, but by pure coincidence she was put in my class, and, fancying my chances, I tried to impress her in lessons. She did not seem to notice me. She was very aloof and much more mature than we boys were. Instead of catching her attention with my jokes, I caught the teacher's attention instead!

"Don't be silly," said my teacher. I hadn't been listening to him while I was busy playing the fool, and I glared at him, thinking he had insulted me. Nobody called me silly.

"Do you know what I said?" he asked me, and I looked at him in silent anger. In front of the whole class he made me stand up and told me that if I had been paying attention in English class instead of flirting, I would have understood what he meant. It was friendly advice, not an insult—he hadn't called me silly, but merely hinted that my behavior was silly.

I felt very humiliated. Everyone laughed at me, including Ugo. I avoided her after that incident for the pure shame of it. It was very painful not to be able to attract the attention of a girl I liked. During my time as a soldier I had been used to booking no refusals, but civilian life was very different. It was difficult to accept that I could not have whatever I wanted.

In town, however, there were women who were always available. I used to go with some of my classmates to "hotels" near the school. There we could smoke and drink and see prostitutes whenever we liked, really giving us the feeling that we had everything. The only problem was the cost, but we found a way around it by telling what we termed at the time "little lies." I could never actually bring myself to lie to my mother outright, so we used to target the parents of my schoolmates instead. If we needed a textbook for school, we would ask them for the money to buy it. However, a new biology textbook by "R.H. Stone and A.B. Cozens" would turn into two books, one by Stone and one by Cozens. Our parents did not know the difference and didn't think to check with the school. They were only too keen to see us get a good education and always found the money for us without question. One of my friends had a father who sold goats in the local marketplace. When we needed money, he often hadn't sold enough goats to give us what we wanted, so we would mercilessly badger him until he was forced to sell his livestock cut-rate just to make a quick buck. We never stopped to think about what a great sacrifice it must have been for him.

We would then take the money and buy marijuana. The "hotels" never asked where our money came from, or how old we were. They didn't care as long as they were making a profit, and we were never denied entry. I saw the prostitutes at the hotel so often that I even had them on credit. Regulars were allowed to keep a tab written down in a little notebook—probably the archetypal "little black book"—where all the nights you spent at the hotel would be recorded. Later on, when I was old enough to leave school and get a job, the women would wait until payday when I would settle my account each month. I was hooked by a very strong, competitive girl who prevented me from seeing any of the other girls at the hotel. A lot of the girls would physically fight in order to keep their clients exclusive, and I confess I was a little intimidated by her.

My friends and I used to sneak out of school for other reasons too. We liked to go to the cinema to watch Bruce Lee films, completely in awe of the wiry and muscular powerhouse fighting his way across the screen. Whenever a popular musician came to town, we would be sure to buy tickets and go to see them in concert. We would even spend our school fees if necessary, just to see the likes of Geraldo Pino, Osibisa, James Brown, or Fela Ransom Kuti. The first time I saw Fela play live in concert I became a massive fan. Of all the musicians and performers that I had ever seen, Fela stood out to me like a beacon of light. He had incredible boldness in his person and a raw honesty in his music that has been seldom surpassed. I still think of him as the single greatest African musician. I decided then that somehow, one day, I would meet him.

My mother never knew that I snuck out of class. She didn't know about the hotels and the marijuana. She didn't even know about the cigarettes. The first time she had caught me smoking, all those years ago, she had made me promise that I would not do it again. Try as I could, I was unable to keep that promise, and it pained me greatly because I loved her so much, and until I drifted away, I had always done everything that would make her happy. In fact, I was considered the perfect child—the "perfect mama's boy" by many of her friends, and she was quite proud of me.

For many years I was able to get away with smoking cigarettes because school was far enough away from home for me to avoid seeing her, but sometimes I would return home for a special visit to tell her how I was getting on and to see how she was. On one of these visits I dressed up smartly and took a picture of myself with my classmates to show her. She was very interested to see the other boys in my class and what my teacher looked like, but as I handed her the photograph she sniffed the air and suddenly grabbed my hand. Immediately she began weeping. She had smelt the odor of stale cigarette smoke on my fingers, and she could see the staining of the nicotine around my nails. She could not possibly know about the drugs, but even the taint of smoking was considered so terrible in our family that I dreaded she would report me to my father. I knelt down at her feet and pleaded with her not to tell him, that I would stop smoking, that I was sorry. Just please not to tell him. She sternly made me get up from the floor. She looked me solemnly in the eye and told me never to kneel down before another human being. "You should only kneel before God," she said. After that episode I took great pains to hide things from my mother. I could not stop myself, but at least I could—if I was careful enough—stop myself hurting her. What she did not know, I thought, could not trouble her.

Many of my visits home were more enjoyable though. I used to go back to participate in the Ekpo Masquerade which was a lot of fun. I preferred this type of masquerade to others ones which required more elaborate initiation rituals of its members, including painful physical endurance trials, libation, indoctrination, and, in some cases, blood sacrifices. I did not feel comfortable being involved with something so strange and secretive that was essentially hand-in-hand with voodoo. The Ekpo just asked for subscription fees, and my father gladly paid them so that I could join in the excitement.

After the civil war, the masquerade enjoyed a brilliant revival in a bid to preserve Igbo culture. It is still performed today, but in a more centralized way in the city. There have been many controls imposed due to unfortunate violence, so the masquerade is now more of a cultural performance than a village rite. As I remember it, masquerade was a time of high spirits and play fighting but never of cold-blooded violence. Each village had their own variation, but there were some universal rules of participation and spectatorship. Only members—and these only men—were allowed to participate in masquerade. The women and the uninitiated had to stay indoors and watch through the windows, or else keep carefully out of the way of the main parade. If they were seen to obstruct the procession in any way, athletic young men would chase them with canes until they ran screaming and laughing to take shelter inside a building. As soon as they were in a "safe house," they would be left alone. Even my own mother was banned from watching the procession when I was to be in it. She threatened to go on strike and not cook me any food that day if I did not let her watch, but I sent her a message to tell her that masquerades need no food!

The village authorities designated a special day for the masquerade. Early in the morning my friends and I would sneak out into the bush and spend several hours gathering leaves and branches to make costumes. We emerged with our waists fringed with foliage, bare-chested, and masked. The drums would be playing ekpo rhythms, the dancing would commence, and we would mill around the procession. Concealing your identity was essential in masquerade, especially from the women. It was important that nobody in the village should recognize you, but for some reason I always failed to mask myself adequately. The girls in the village said that they could tell who I was just by the way I walked. Keeping to etiquette, they did not say my name out loud—this would have ruined the masquerade, effectively unmasking me and breaking the illusion. Masquerade is the tradition of enacting the spirits of animals, of tribal gods, of our ancestors, and allowing them free passage through the village. It is important, then, that we should not be hindered, because when dressed up and masked, we carried the spirits through. The spirits always had the right of way. The girls respected this, and those who could not help themselves simply called out, "Ekpo Guy! Ekpo Guy!," to show that they had seen me. Try as I might, I could never escape detection, and the chanting would fill the air as I walked by. The girls said that I had a way of adding glamor to the proceedings, and I would be forever thought of as the "stylish masquerade."

People who obstructed the procession were dealt with quite harshly. Everybody in the village knew the rules, but sometimes there would be somebody from out of town who failed to show the proper respect. I remember coming across a boy who stood right in the path of the parade, watching us approach. I sent a messenger ahead to ask him to step aside as he was in our way. He said he had been standing there for some time, and he didn't see why he shouldn't stay there. It didn't matter if other people had moved—*he* wasn't going anywhere. I was outraged by his lack of respect. He wasn't an initiate. He wasn't even local. He was on holiday in our village from Aba, and did not even have the decency to respect our customs. As I passed him, I touched him with some embers I was carrying as a torch. He was burnt badly enough to learn his lesson, and he was taken back to Aba never to visit again.

In the heat and excitement of masquerade it was easy to lose one's temper, and I did not mean to cause him serious harm. Generally it was acceptable to singe the clothes of those who were disrespectful. We could also chase people away with our brandished canes, although this was usually reserved for girls. The playful "harassment" was traditionally part of the masquerade, and it was also chance to get your revenge on any girl who had spurned your advances or played hard to get. The girls would not know who the perpetrators were because they were all masked, so there could be no complaints afterward, but it was all done in a spirit of fun, and nobody was seriously injured. In Nigeria's male-centered culture, it was considered perfectly normal that the initiated men should take precedence like this and exact a playful tyranny over the women of the village. Things are changing, but Nigeria is still very much a patriarchal society. Although a deep respect exists for women as mothers, the treatment of women in general still leaves a lot to be desired, and I suppose I just unquestioningly accepted the patriarchal way of things as I grew up.

THE MAGICIAN

1973 heralded a strange period in my life. My parents began living apart, as some of my father's relatives had been plotting to separate them and had finally succeeded in influencing my father. My father trusted their advice, and because he was so compliant and unsuspecting, it was a long time before he saw through their lies. I never knew exactly what they told him, but it was sufficient for him to abandon his wife and all his children, forcing my mother to live alone in Aba and bring up my sisters and brothers single-handedly. As far as I know, my father never married or lived with another woman during this time. He lived alone in Owerri and suffered years of being separated from his family. His relatives prevented my mother from ever seeing him. I felt frustrated that I was not older, as there was nothing I could do to bring my parents back together. I had to wait many years before I was able to influence the situation and reunite them.

We had been forced to move into a room in a house shared with many other families, within a large compound. There was one toilet and washroom for everybody in the house, and it was not uncommon for over forty people to have to share the facilities, as there were often over ten people per room. Our room housed my mother, me, my six brothers and sisters, and my mother's younger brother who had nowhere else to live. Mother kept us all fed and clothed by trading, but she had to work extremely hard in order to earn a pittance.

Now that I had finished school, I tried to relieve my mother of the burden of supporting me by getting a job. I didn't have any particular job in mind, so when I saw an advert for negotiators at the Nigerian Amicable Assurance Company in Aba, I applied. There weren't very many career possibilities at that time. I didn't fancy going into teaching as I didn't have the vocation, so I settled instead on a course which I thought would make me a bit of money quite quickly. I was very naïve. What I didn't realize when I applied was that the job relied entirely on commission. There was no basic salary. This allowed the company to have lots of sales representatives on hand to advertise the company and talk to people about the insurance products on offer, but unless we personally closed the deal, we would not get any money for our work. We got no training or advice to help us with our work, so time and time again, other, older men, who had been there longer, would get the clients to sign on the dotted line, and the younger recruits would be left out in the cold.

After a few months of hanging around the local motor licensing office, trying in vain to persuade passing drivers to buy car insurance, I began to get disheartened. The only deal I actually made was with a family friend, who felt sorry for me and allowed me to arrange insurance for his vehicle. Instead of making my own way and supporting my mother, it turned out that going to work each day, providing lunch and suitable business clothes, actually cost her more than ever before! I felt terrible about it and desperately looked about me for a way of improving my lot. Suddenly, the answer seemed to appear right before my eyes.

I had gotten to know the guys who hung out at the licensing office, as there was quite a regular crowd of us, and a man from another company befriended me. I used to chat to him about how business was going, and he used to ask me about my colleagues, the competition, my ambitions, etc. I must have told him a lot about myself, without realizing that I knew almost nothing about him. Nevertheless, when he suggested that I come and see his friend who might be able to help me improve my sales, I went along quite willingly.

His friend was called Sunny, and I was taken to meet him at his house in town. In the corner of his front room he had a rather impressive temple where he sat to receive visitors. This temple booth was decked out in reams of bright red cotton; strange icons hung from the walls, and the whole place exuded strong-smelling incense. It had a vaguely religious feel to it, mixed with black magic, and inside he had collected several of the Books of Moses to add an imposing backdrop to his consultations. These books were magical texts purporting to instruct the reader in the ways of bringing about biblical miracles. He was holding one as I entered the booth, and began murmuring some of the incantations on the page, but he would not let me get a look at the book or go behind the red curtains, which demarcated the sacred boundary of the inner sanctum.

I suppose you could say Sunny was a magician, but he dressed normally, and nothing about his person marked him out as such. He relied on his homemade temple business and his overwhelmingly persuasive presence to impress his clients. Trusting my newfound friend, it was some time before I realized that I was, effectively, his client.

At the end of the meeting, it was revealed that a little consultation fee was required, which Sunny said he needed in order to make the magic work effectively in my favor. He "diagnosed" my problem without much trouble. Apparently an aunt and an uncle of mine had put a spell on me to curse my potential at work. What was needed was a charm to break the power of their spell and cancel the bad luck, and then a further charm to bring me good luck.

I could well believe that relatives of my father would wish ill luck on his children after how they had behaved toward my mother, so I accepted his explanation without reservation. After taking my money, he told me to return to his house that night and booked me an official appointment to have the bad spell broken. This was to be highly secretive, and for fear of angering the gods, I was made to promise not to tell a soul about it. Sunny said that if I broke my promise, the person I loved the most would die. A fear for my mother's life gripped me with horror, and I would not have revealed my secret for anything in the world. This was yet another secret that I was forced to keep from her, and it troubled me greatly. I had promised always to be honest with her and tell her everything. Nevertheless, the desire I had to get on in my job and earn some money to rescue her from poverty spurred me on. I kept my secret appointment very secret.

I met Sunny that night around midnight outside his house. He emerged with my insurance friend in tow, and together they brought me to a large cemetery. Sunny told me that it was essential to commune with the spirits, and they would decide how we should combat the evil forces at work against me. I was made to kneel down in the dark, on a large, flat gravestone. Sunny said it was imperative that I keep my eyes closed throughout the visit to avoid offending the spirits. I screwed my eyelids shut, and felt the cold stone grazing my knees. They left me by the grave, saying I needed to be alone if this was to work. Apparently a spirit would speak to me, and give me its wisdom. I just had to wait to hear its voice.

I waited for some minutes by myself in the dark. I felt cold and uncomfortable on the tombstone, and my mind was uneasy. Suddenly a voice started calling me by name.

"Lawrence," it called softly, "Lawrence, do you want to see me?"

"No!" I cried loudly, "No, I don't want to see you!" I was terrified at the prospect of seeing a ghost, and I did not want the spirit to reveal itself to me. Again and again, it asked me if I would like it to come out of the grave, and repeatedly, I begged it not to come near me. I was so afraid I began to shake. I began to pray in a whisper, desperate for protection. I kept my eyes tightly closed so as not to see the thing if it did decide to emerge from the tomb, and mumbled in the affirmative when it asked if I wanted its help.

It then proceeded to tell me all about the problems I was having at work, the strain on my family, the curse that was preventing me from earning money. I was amazed that it should know everything about me, and I listened intently for what seemed like ages. Eventually, it said that I was released from the spell, and that I could go home. Then there was silence. In the darkness I waited to see if there would be more voices, but there was nothing. I opened my eyes warily, and I was alone on top of the gravestone. I breathed a sigh of relief, and my hammering heart slowly returned to normal.

Sunny and my friend escorted me to his house where they impressed on me once again the necessity of not telling anyone about my experience on pain of death. I was so afraid by that point that I would have done anything they asked of me. My sales over the next few weeks, however, did not improve. I was no more successful than before, and I began to doubt that the spirit had really helped at all. I could not afford to go back to Sunny just yet, so I decided to bide my time. Perhaps I did not have enough patience.

As the weeks slid by, my work continued to yield no return, and one day I discovered that the little bit of emergency money I had was gone. My mother's brother suggested that my brother Samuel—due to visit our grandmother for his school holidays—might have taken it in order to have a bit of extra pocket money. I was so angry that I ran all the way to the bus station in order to catch him before he boarded the bus to Enugu. Despite his protestations of innocence, I furiously ripped open his suitcase, almost strip-searching him in my determination to find the money. It was not there.

Not knowing who else to accuse, I turned to Sunny for help, believing that he could identify the perpetrator. My cousin Stanley, who was on holiday and staying with us at the time, accompanied me to the exotic red temple at Sunny's house. After listening to my plight, Sunny retired immediately into the back room to consult with his gods, lighting candles on the altar and, after a reverential pause, bringing out a blank sheet of paper. He handed me another piece of paper and instructed me to burn it over a candle, which I duly did. Next, I had to rub the charred paper over the blank sheet Sunny had provided. Immediately a name appeared magically out of the black mark left by the ashes. It was the name of my cousin, Stanley.

I could not believe my eyes. Stanley had arrived just days before the money went missing. He would have had the opportunity, yes, but his family was reasonably well off, and I knew that he would never steal from anyone. I began to doubt Sunny's methods, but could not offer another explanation. Stanley glared at me in anger, insulted that he should be accused of being a petty thief. We went home, and he said he wanted to show me something. He went through the same ritual as Sunny, lighting the candles, bringing out the blank piece of paper, and getting me to burn another one. This time, when I rubbed the burnt paper onto the clean sheet, my own name appeared out of the ashes.

All of a sudden I realized that all Sunny had actually done was to write a name in wax on the paper, which was then brought out in relief when the ashes were rubbed over it. In the relative gloom of the curtained booth, the trick had been impossible to spot. I questioned my mother's brother again about the money. He had falsely accused my brother of stealing it, and I figured that this was in order to direct suspicion away from his own guilt. He returned the money without a fuss. I decided to have nothing more to do with Sunny. The showmanship had convinced me—the books of Moses, the candles, the incense, the elaborate rituals—and my desperation to make money had blinded me to the emptiness of the charade. The clever setup in the graveyard, which had scared me half to death, had been achieved with just a couple of loudspeakers and a disguised voice. In my fear of bringing death or curses on my family (this belief is still very strong in Nigeria, in spite of Christianity), I had believed everything.

My so-called "friend" at the motor licensing office became quite aggressive after that. He said that I would be cursed if I did not continue to give Sunny payment for the services he had rendered. When I told him I knew all about their scam, he and Sunny threatened to kill me, probably scared that I would ruin their lucrative con business by telling everyone it was a sham. It was partly due to these threats that I left Aba, although I also wanted a change of scene. I wasn't going anywhere with the insurance company, and I was tired of being a hanger-on. It seemed like a good time to skip town.

Chapter Four

CONSCIENCE AND CORRUPTION

Quite by chance a family friend was driving to Lagos that week, and he asked me to be his companion during the trip. I had never been to Lagos before, and he thought it would be an exciting experience for me. It took around eight hours from Aba, stopping en route to see a friend at the University of Ibadan. I had always wanted to go on to higher education, but I felt that I had missed the boat. By the time I got enough money together to afford the course, my fellow students would be young enough to be my children!

So on this road trip, with money worries always in the back of my mind, I was keeping an eye out for a possible career. I saw this little jaunt to Lagos as a holiday between jobs, time to think and plan my next move. It was also an immediate relief from the constant harassment of Sunny and his gang. I looked forward to the excitement of Lagos with a peculiar intensity. It was a sort of no-man's-land—rich, plentiful, but also quite lawless and dangerous, different from all other Nigerian cities. It was like going abroad, except there were no immigration restrictions, and you didn't need a passport. There was the freedom there to do what you liked, become a different person, indulge your every desire—but you had to think on your feet and fend for yourself. Nobody will take care of you. This is Lagos, a city on the edge. It was also the home of my idol, Fela Kuti.

I honestly hadn't planned to do what I did. The idea just came to me, spontaneously, after seeing Fela perform at the Afrika Shrine. My family friend had booked us in at the same hotel that hosted the Shrine as its club venue, where Fela habitually played. One night, after my friend was in bed, I couldn't resist sneaking downstairs to hear the music. Guests of the hotel were allowed in free, which was just as well as I didn't have any money. The effect of that night on me was electric. I watched Fela from close range, drinking in the audacity of his performance, his movement, his sinewy body, his powerful voice, all mixed with the intoxicating rhythms of his band and the sensual dancing of his numerous, beautiful girlfriends. He commanded his musicians like an audio army. Just a flick of his hand and they would start playing. Master of the stage, he would stalk about with his dancers like a lion with his pride. I bathed in his confidence and assurance. It seemed my prayers had been granted. I had longed to see him again, but had not thought it would be possible, and now that the unthinkable had happened, I realized this was my only chance to meet him. I seized the opportunity of talking to some of the band members and entourage as they milled around the club, each new contact inching me slowly toward the man himself.

When I woke up the next morning, I realized that I had to act fast. We only had five days in Lagos, and our time was up. I knew I had an uncle somewhere in Lagos, but I hadn't seen him for years. Not letting this deter me, I looked him up and went to see him in the district of Suru-Lere. I confessed that I didn't want to go home, but that I had nowhere to stay, and he kindly gave me a place to sleep. I never went back to the hotel, not knowing how to tell my family friend, who was expecting me to drive back with him that night. Not knowing where to find me, my friend was forced to leave without me. He had seen that I had taken all my things from the hotel room and came to the conclusion that I had planned the whole thing, using him as my means of escape from the East. On his return to Aba he accused my mother of colluding with me, encouraging me to get a free ride to Lagos and find work there. Of course my mother knew nothing about it, but our friend was convinced and became so incensed that he cut off all contact with my family. He felt he had been very ill-used—which of course he had, but not by my poor mother!

I enjoyed my escapade immensely. With my new contacts, I was able to get into the Africa Shrine almost every night to watch Fela perform, and I was able to get hold of marijuana for nothing, thanks to their generosity. There was also nothing to fear from the authorities. I saw policemen and soldiers openly buying marijuana in the street—and even sitting down and smoking it in public. Opposite the Shrine stood Fela's self-proclaimed independent state, the Kalakuta Republic, a commune housing him and his many wives, girlfriends, friends, and band members. I now knew many people who lived in the Republic and was quite good friends with several of Fela's musicians, but I still couldn't break through the barrier which prevented me from being anything more than a fan. After months of giddy freedom, I had to face up to reality. Without a job, without money, Lagos was not a permanent option, and it was with a heavy heart that I knew I must return, for the moment, to Aba. I felt an invisible cord entwined my life with Fela's, but for the moment he was just beyond my reach.

THE BATON OF HONOR

Once back in Aba, I learnt that the Nigerian Police Force was recruiting. I attended their open day with high hopes, only to find that my chest measurement did not meet their standards. Needing to increase my chest from 32 to 34 inches, I began a rigorous daily exercise program, lifting weights and doing push-ups. At the next recruitment day, I did not fall short. Sunny and his friends were still lurking on the scene, and after my return from Lagos, I had been keeping a pretty low profile. It was partly a need for empowerment that inspired me to join the police. As an officer of the law, Sunny would not dare touch me. I would finally be free of him.

I was enlisted and signed on for a year's training at the Police College. These days our policemen are trained for just a couple of months, and half of them can't even handle a rifle by the time they are put on active service! At the time I joined up, trainee recruits were required to pass monthly examinations in three areas: class work, parade, and range (shooting practice). I was smaller than all the other recruits in spite of my personal efforts to increase my muscles, and I attracted the notice of the Assistant Police Commissioner. She looked me over and declared that she did not think I would survive the training. Not one to give up easily, I decided to prove her wrong, and I threw myself into my training with determination.

It was tough. The exercises were grueling; we had to get up extremely early for drill and parade work, and physical stamina was pushed to the limit. My arms and legs ached horribly, I could barely move by the time I crawled into bed at night. After the first week, two thirds of the recruits had dropped out, probably having quickly realized that it was not going to be an easy ride. I was really passionate about being in the police force. Not only did I seek the power and freedom that came with the uniform and the position, but I also sought to give myself a steady income and the freedom to travel all over the country. It might just get me a ticket back to Lagos.

If a recruit maintained first position in all three areas of examination for the duration of the training, then he would earn the Baton of Honor, the first prize. This was the aim of everyone there, as it meant that your first promotion after graduation would shoot you straight up to the role of Inspector of

Police, skipping over the ranks of Corporal and Sergeant. The atmosphere was highly competitive. I exerted myself and managed to gain top marks in all my exams each month, earning me the title of Squad Leader. This gave me the responsibility of delegating tasks to the team, exempting me from all chores. Obviously, this privileged position was wholly dependent on consistent distinction in exams, and I needed to work hard to maintain my grades in order to keep it. My desire to stay Squad Leader each month motivated me to excel throughout the year, and I never relinquished the title. At the end of the year, my name was engraved in the recreation room at the college in recognition of my achievement as recipient of the prestigious Baton of Honor.

I hoped and prayed that I would be allowed to return to Lagos. A policeman was not allowed to refuse a posting, so your place of work after graduation was purely the luck of the draw. We were given our Force Numbers, and we nervously awaited our posting. Our names were called out, one by one, and then our destination. Only three people were to be sent to Lagos, and I was one of them. I couldn't believe my luck! Still dazed from the news, I was handed my ticket. We all piled into a car and were taken to the train station at Enugu for immediate departure.

The journey seemed interminable, as I couldn't wait to reach Lagos. The train line ran north before heading south again, and we made many stops en route to allow our fellow recruits to go off to their various postings in Kafanchan or Ibadan. My impatience had reached record levels when the train we were on had to stop. The driver told us that there had been a derailment up ahead, and it was not possible to continue. We got off at the nearest station and waited.

For three days and nights we waited for them to clear the train tracks so that we could get on our way. There was nothing to do in the town, nowhere to go, and we had run out of marijuana. My colleagues all smoked weed, but were reluctant to go out and buy some, as it would risk their reputation. They claimed that it was impossible to get some in this town anyway, but I told them that I could root some out no problem, especially since my craving for a high was reaching epic proportions. Less than two hours later I returned with a stash, to the amazement of all. They were quite happy to share it with me, but next time I insisted we all go out on the hunt together. On day three we returned from buying weed just in time to hear the news that the train lines had been cleared and our train was due to leave any minute. We sprinted down to the station and got on board with seconds to spare.

We arrived in Lagos on a bright Saturday morning with the whole weekend before us, not having to report for duty until eight o'clock on Monday. My former experience of the city gave me the upper hand with my new colleagues, and I was able to show them round. They were impressed with my knowledge, especially when I knew exactly where to buy weed and meet cool musicians. I went up several notches in their estimation and felt like a lord.

Monday morning rolled around, and I turned up for my first assignment at the Lagos State Police Command Headquarters on Lagos Island. My high spirits were quickly dampened. There were no introductions; there was no time for chatting. We were sent out on active duty immediately. My assignment did not even have the benefit of company—I was told to go it alone, with a Mark Four rifle for backup. My task was to intervene in the disagreement between two groups of Muslims who were disputing the right of the other to worship at a certain mosque in the city. A woman had been murdered in the clash, and in fear of punishment, the group responsible kept trying to kidnap the body in order to burn the evidence against them. My less than enviable job was to guard the corpse until the forensic team arrived on the scene. If it went missing, my sergeant informed me, then he would make sure that I would also go missing.

The forensic people certainly took their time about it. The corpse was decomposing at a rapid rate in the heat, and the stench was becoming unbearable. I had no breaks, nothing to eat or drink, and yet I was expected to remain alert. I could hardly blink. Every time anybody came within a hundred yards of the body, I shouted at them and threatened to shoot if they did not leave. My voice became hoarse with all the yelling, and my throat was parched. It was not until four o'clock in the afternoon that the police doctor and photographer arrived, by which time the corpse did not look at all like it had done that morning. It was another few hours before I was relieved, though. I still had to wait around for the local government officials to come and remove the body to the morgue. As a first assignment, it was pretty tough, but it curbed my fear and made me ready for anything. On the other hand, it immediately made me reconsider my choice to be a policeman.

Based at a Police Station in Lagos, I quickly became used to the ways of the Force. After the Civil War, the crime rate in Nigeria was particularly high, and Lagos was a microcosm. Huge numbers of people unemployed and displaced by civil unrest had flocked to the city. Money was hard to come by, but guns were plentiful, so we had a lot of armed robberies. Many policemen lost their lives at this time due to trigger-happy felons, and the police policy of not shooting first. We did not have enough protection from our equipment, so when we were on duty, we would team up with a nearby army patrol. This helped enormously during shoot-outs with armed gangs, which inevitably happened before we were able to arrest anybody.

Then there was the corruption. My station was probably the one of the most corrupt stations in the city. I remember several incidents which stood out for me as prime examples of the inherent lack of justice in our police force. I had been made Inspector of Police pretty quickly, due to my performance at training college. One morning I heard a complaint made by a man against his landlord. In order to investigate the claim further, I sent a couple of my men to visit the landlord, a wealthy man, and "invite" him to come down to the station for questioning. If he had been poor, we would have arrested him first and questioned him afterward, but money speaks strongly in Nigeria. The men arrived back at the station empty-handed: to my surprise, the man had declined our "invitation." I went to his house myself, and after some time persuaded him to come and give a formal statement. He refused to accompany us in the police car, but instead insisted on driving there in his white Mercedes.

The complainant was still there, waiting patiently. We took the landlord into the boss's office to avoid confrontation, and my boss interviewed him alone. The whole discussion did not take more than thirty minutes, by which time the landlord had left the station and driven off. My boss came out of the room and pointed to the complainant who was still sitting, waiting expectantly.

"Lock this man up," he said.

"But sir," I replied incredulously, "This man is the complainant!"

He looked at me. He was not used to people arguing with him. "Inspector Oji, I told you to lock this man in the cell."

I saluted him with due deference to his rank, and then repeated my statement. This did not please him at all, and he became very angry. "Inspector Oji," he said, "Are you trying to teach me my job? If you will not obey orders and put this man in the cell, then you will go into the cell in his place."

"Sir," I replied indignantly, "I would rather go into the cell than put this man in the cell."

He was red in the face. All the other police officers had gone silent. He looked around, needing to save face. "Then you go inside the cell," he said, and walked off.

I asked "Writer Two," the cell warden, to let me in himself. I handed him my beret and my badge to show my respect for the police force—as we were taught in Police College—and went in, prepared to stay the night if necessary. My boss was shocked. He had never expected disobedience from me, but I refused to let an innocent man suffer for blowing the whistle on a corrupt landlord. He could have been in there for months, too poor to bail himself out and with no friends or relations rich enough to help him. People who did not pay their bail money often ended up in court and were put in remand, regardless of their innocence and the lack of evidence against them. Many people lost their minds in this long, painfully unfair process. Fortunately for me, I was not kept overnight. My boss sent for me after a few hours and reminded me of the O.B.C. code: Obey Before Complaint. In front of all my colleagues, I was sent home for the rest of the day for insubordination. In spite of this humiliation, I did not regret doing the right thing.

Sadly, there were many cases like this. I remember a young boy who was arrested for "wandering" in his neighborhood after dark. This vague charge could be used on anyone walking around at night, or sometimes even during the day if a policeman did not like the look of what you were doing. It was an easy way of extorting a bribe. The boy was hardly a vagrant—he lived right across the road! He had only gone out to borrow a book from a friend while studying for his GCE exams and was returning with the book when the police picked him up. He ended up in the cells, with no money to bail himself out. When I came on duty later that evening, I found him sobbing by himself in a corner. Having found out what happened, I was determined to secure his release. I made repeated calls to my District Police Officer until he came down himself to order that the poor boy be set free. The whole experience was very traumatic for him, and I can only hope that he passed his exams after all the trouble caused by obtaining that fateful textbook.

Apart from arresting people on the scantiest of charges, it was common for policemen to conduct unofficial "stop-and-searches." If we didn't find what we were looking for—be it drugs, counterfeit money, stolen goods, contraband alcohol, or simply an unregistered license plate on the car—we would plant it on the suspect or invent it. In order to avoid being arrested, they would then have to pay up, and we got what we wanted. Easy money. This worked in many situations, including ones where we actually had a real tip-off about unlawful activity. Often the suspects would get wind of the plot and would hide or even destroy their stash, but we would always be ready with something to plant as evidence.

This appalling corruption funded our drug habit, as practically all police officers smoked marijuana, often coupled with hard drugs. The fact was so well known that it affected the outcome of one of our cases. We had raided the premises of a marijuana dealer as retaliation for an insult he had given one of my colleagues. He escaped, leaving an enormous quantity of weed behind, so we appropriated it. We sent word that for a small fee we would give him back his drugs (the value of which was quite significant) and hush up the raid, but he failed to appear at the police station by the deadline we had allotted him. Thinking he was going to abandon the drugs altogether, we ended up officially reporting the raid, despite promising him it would remain off the record.

He turned up to collect the drugs eventually, thinking that we had kept our end of the bargain. We took the bribe, not wanting to admit we had bungled it, but the fact remained that once reported, an incident could not be erased from the logbook. In order to rectify the situation, we took the drug sample which was to be submitted as evidence in the case and (ingeniously, we thought) substituted normal grass from the police station yard for it. Thinking that would solve the problem, we couldn't have been more surprised when the results actually came back as positive for marijuana! The forensic lab obviously did not believe for a minute that policemen from that notorious station would not know the difference between grass and *grass*. So the case proceeded to trial, and the drug dealer was furious that he had paid his bribe for nothing.

This fiasco had other repercussions as well, as reports of the attempted cover-up reached those higher in command. It exposed the complicity of police officers in the supply and trafficking of drugs, especially marijuana. At my station, even the prisoners in the cells had access to drugs through the officers who were supposed to be guarding them. For a small bribe, as well as the main payment, wardens would peddle all kinds of drugs. Policemen made a lot of extra cash that way. The fake evidence incident led to a massive transfer of all the officers involved. Fortunately, I got to stay on at the same station. Ringleaders were moved to other stations as punishment, away from their colleagues, but to my knowledge, nobody actually got fired for attempting to pervert the course of justice. The cover-up operation just triggered a bigger cover-up within the police force itself.

I gradually grew tired of the police force. It was not what I hoped it would be. I hated the violence, and I hated the corruption, although I was a part of it. I was often told that I was "too nice" to be a policeman. I never succeeded fully in switching off my conscience, and even little incidents like the boy and his textbook began to weigh heavily on me. After the initial elation of my graduation, I felt absolutely no pride in my job. Most people feared and despised policemen, even hated them. My friends had no idea where I worked, because a lot of them would not talk to me if they knew. Few of my colleagues knew what sort of company I kept outside work. I led a sort of double life. On the one side I was a policeman. On the other side, I was the devoted friend and servant of Fela Kuti.

Chapter Five

A DOUBLE LIFE

I lived for Fela. My days began and ended at the Afrika Shrine, where I would hang out before and after work. It was strange to separate the two parts of my life, but necessary. Fela's tireless championing of minority rights and freedom for Africans everywhere was inspirational, but controversial. His powerful lyrics often enraged the Nigerian government, containing direct attacks on policy and corruption within the state. Even today, Fela is still a sort of taboo subject in Nigeria. His music and the story of his life still have the power to threaten Nigerian politics. As a policeman, I was supposed to uphold the status quo, but it was Fela's beliefs that formed my creed, and I found it increasingly difficult to serve two masters with such opposing ideals. Outside of work, my appearance began to resemble his. I took to wearing nothing but pants around the house, like he did at home , and I openly kept a tray of marijuana in my lounge, much to my mother's disapproval. I even adopted the Black Power salute which was Fela's trademark greeting. In my attitude, I tried to mirror Fela's honesty and his unashamed free-and-easy lifestyle. At work, though, I was still what Fela would term a "zombie," a servant of the state.

Fela's band, the Africa '70, played at least four times a week at the Shrine. I would go to watch, each time looking for ways to get close to Fela. Even at rehearsals there would be several hundred people watching, wanting to be part of the music. I had many friends amongst his group of followers, and eventually I began to seize small opportunities to say a few words to my idol. I was at the Shrine so often that I became part of his "camp," the swarm of people always buzzing around the great man. Much to my joy, we gradually became firm friends, and I was often a visitor at his house in the commune of the Kalakuta Republic. My love and admiration for the man only grew the more I got to know him on a personal level. I refused to believe that he could be wrong on any subject, and I took his word as law. I wanted everyone to know that I was a loyal follower, and to show this, I accompanied him everywhere. My other friends were very envious, especially as I could not quite explain how I became close to Fela. It was just one of those things I had known would eventually happen.

February 18, 1977, was the day that changed everything. I was at the Lion Building headquarters when the bugle sounded. There was no briefing, but we were ordered to remove our badges and personal identification numbers from our uniform. This was clearly in anticipation of a cover-up. We were rushed into jeeps and driven downtown without being informed of our destination. I will never forget the sight which greeted me there.

A large house was on fire, the flames leaping toward the sky. It was the middle of the day, and the heat was immense. People were screaming for help from the upper windows, but nobody went forward to assist them. They couldn't get downstairs because soldiers had poured petrol all over the carpets on the ground floor. It was an inferno, and the smoke billowed in great, black, choking clouds. Hundreds of soldiers surrounded the building. Whenever anybody managed to leap to the ground from the upper stories, they would grab hold of them and start beating them, even if they were already badly burned. The house was the Kalakuta Republic, and the victims were my friends. I felt sick and devastated, but there was nothing I could do. I wanted to help, but there were just too many policemen and soldiers—and they were all on the side of the "law."

Then, with horror, I saw Fela's mother. She was crying out from the window, trapped on the first floor. Whether she jumped or was thrown I don't know, but I watched her fall from the window and hit the ground, lying there unconscious. Her leg was broken. She was left there for a long time. The soldiers set fire to the whole compound, and everything was destroyed. Much of Fela's music, the recording studio, his cars and furniture, the movie he had made (an anti-government film entitled, *The Black President*)—everything went up in smoke. The wounded were taken to hospital, including Fela's mother and brother. His mother's injuries were fatal. Fela himself was badly beaten by the soldiers, and we thought he was dead. He was dragged out, bleeding and naked. They had ripped his clothes from him.

As a sort of sick joke, the police station assigned me the job of guarding Fela in hospital. They knew that I admired him, and they wanted me to see him laid low. It was their idea of a punishment. They had broken his knee, his shoulder, and his ankles; they had gashed his head and bruised his face. He looked terrible, but he remained strong and defiant. Nothing could break his spirit. As I entered the room, he took one look at my uniform and used his good arm to attempt to lift his crutches and beat me with them.

"Zombie," he said, contemptuously.

Quickly I raised my hand and made a black power salute, saying, "Fela, I'm your friend. I'm always at the Shrine." I took a packet of marijuana from my breast pocket and gave it to him as an offering.

He accepted it graciously, but said, "You're still a zombie, but a zombie with ideology."

Fela wanted to know how his mother was. She had been taken to a different hospital, and the police were preventing him from having any contact with her or the rest of his family. This was my chance to assuage my conscience, and I offered to be his errand boy. This is how I got my nickname "Solution," because I would fix problems for people. Unbeknownst to my superiors, I carried messages to his family, passed them notes written by Fela, and brought him a steady supply of marijuana to ease his pain. I did everything I could to make it up to him. I felt so terrible about what he had had to suffer.

I was supposed to stay all night at the hospital to guard him. "Do you think I'll escape from hospital?" He asked, jokingly, waving his crutches. I admitted there was not much chance of that, so I left him alone while I went home and slept. It was a while before he was released from hospital. His breaks never fully healed, and he always walked with a limp. It did not, however, detract from his incredible stage presence or prevent him from performing. He was unstoppable. His energy was irrepressible.

After the fire, he stayed at the Crossroad Hotel while he looked for another place to live. I lived with him there as we had become very close, and I loved his company. He was officially banned from performing, but we secretly arranged a show anyway at City Hall. We rented the venue in another name, but in spite of having the receipt, the place was stormed by police, and Fela was prevented from playing. When he began to perform again at the Shrine on a regular basis, the crowd would always have one ear open for the sound of police at the door. On one occasion there was a stampede when somebody thought he heard the police. In spite of the confusion, Fela did not bat an eyelid, and the band kept playing. I stayed where I was. Fela had taught me that man should not be afraid of other men. He once wrote a song called, "Fear, Not for Man." It was his philosophy. He was so courageous, and I wished I could be that strong.

When his mother died as a result of the injuries she sustained on the day of the fire, he placed her coffin on the steps of the Capitol building, demanding that the government step up and take responsibility for what they had done to his family and friends. At the same time he released a song called, "Coffin for Head of State"—maximum impact. Of course there was no apology, no admittance of guilt from the State, but the action of protest was duly noted. The government said they would hold an enquiry into the fire, and many of those involved were called upon to give testimony.

I jumped at the chance to tell everybody what really happened, and on the day of the inquest I went to the National Theater and stated exactly what I had seen. I held nothing back, even stating that I had seen soldiers deliberately burning the house and jeopardizing the lives of those inside. I said that these soldiers were directly responsible for the death of Fela's mother. I stayed for the verdict, wanting to hear the words of justice spoken, and to my surprise the inquest ruled that the whole episode had been the fault of an "unknown soldier" (this inspired the title of another protest album by Fela). One imaginary, renegade soldier was used as a scapegoat! Now I knew why our identification badges had been removed. There was no way of pinning down any of the culprits, and of course, nobody was charged with the crime.

I left the theater feeling very downcast. I had told the truth, but it had been disregarded by the very people who were supposed to be upholding justice in our country. As I came out of the main doors, I was seized by several military policemen. What I had not banked on was the reaction of the State. For a policeman to testify against the government was actually an offence punishable by a prison sentence. I had naively thought that the commission set up to investigate the fire was a serious one which would come to a fair judgment. I should have known that it was all for show. My role as a policeman was merely to back up whatever the government chose as their line, not to expose their failings. I was sick of the whole thing. My loyalty was firmly with Fela, and if the police force was against him, then I wanted no part of it. I started to look for a way out. My faith in Fela was not misplaced. As soon as he heard that I had been arrested, he sent his lawyer to assist me. This lawyer was extremely well connected, and in less than a few hours he had managed to obtain my release.

Fela had many thousands of admirers around the world, but his enemies in Nigeria would spread rumors of immorality and perversion. Some rather extraordinary things he did were deliberately misinterpreted and used against him. He came under fire for his conduct with women—after the destruction of the Kalakuta Republic, he married twenty-seven women on the same day. The State said this was to use them as his harem, but he believed he was protecting them by offering them a home and status. Many of the women had lived in the Kalakuta Republic and now had nowhere else to go. Fela openly used Indian hemp, which was regarded with suspicion (being stronger and more potent than regular cannabis), but he never used hard drugs. I remember offering him heroin once, after I had first started using it, and he said to me, "Solution, why do you want to use something which will not allow you to enjoy women?" He had a strict belief that anything other than cannabis would affect your sex life, and have a negative effect on life in general. In fact, he banned hard drugs from the Shrine (although some people, including me, flouted this rule).

My family knew of Fela's reputation and were naturally concerned about me associating with "that kind of man," so really I shouldn't have been all that surprised when I got home one day to find my mother sitting in my living room. Since she rarely came down to Lagos due to the grueling eight-hour journey, and certainly never made impromptu visits, I immediately attributed the visit to troubles at home. I worried that my father might be ill. When I asked her what was wrong, she replied that everything was fine, and that my father sent his greetings. I breathed a sigh of relief, but she suddenly burst out, "What is this I am hearing about you going about with that musician called Fela?"

I did not know what to say to this, but I was not about to say anything against Fela. "There are many people talking back home about you associating with this madman." Some of the rumors she had heard were quite terrible, and she was very ashamed that her son should be connected in any way with such a person. She had decided to come to Lagos and confront me about it, and ask me to end my association with Fela.

"And *this* is why you came?" I asked her, surprised. There was nothing I wanted to say about Fela. I didn't feel the need to defend him, or my friendship with him. I knew that she was acting on mere hearsay. The only thing to do was to introduce my mother to him so that she could make up her own mind. I was sure she would like him.

I didn't tell her we were going to visit Fela, but instead took her on a tour of the city, showing her the new airport, the National Theater, and Tafawa Balewa Square with its proud, rearing horses and red eagles. We made our way to Ikeja, where Fela was now staying, and it was not until we were inside the compound gates and people greeted me with shouts of "Olopa" (Policeman) that she realized where we were. By then it was too late to retreat, and she clung to me as we walked into the house. In the living room, a large crowd had gathered so that there was no room to sit down anywhere. Fela sat in a very relaxed attitude in a large armchair, wearing just a pair of briefs. He was holding court. He did this regularly, assisting people with decisions and settling disputes like the kings of old used to do. His attention would appear to be elsewhere, but at the end of the plaintiff's story, he would always pass judgment accordingly.

My mother was impressed by his wisdom and impartiality, and whispered to me, "Lawrence, this man is indeed a genius."

"No, Mom," I replied, sarcastically, "He is a madman!"

There were some white men present, but with deference they waited until the court session was over before presenting their own matter. It turned out that they were there to ask him to take part in the 1978 Berlin Jazz Festival as a special guest artist, but he did not give them precedence. White or black, he treated everyone the same.

Looking back now, I do not regret my association with Fela. He was a great man, and I learned many positive things from him. Most of all, his music and outspokenness endeared him to me and to Africa's poor. Here was a man who was fearless; he was not afraid to stand up for what he believed in; he was a tornado of a man who liked to play, eat, love women, and get high on marijuana. But he was also sweet—he loved humanity, and he was principled. This was what won him people's admiration, including mine.

My admiration for Fela in today's world could be likened to the admiration of our youths for celebrities such as musicians, soccer stars, movie stars, and so on. This admiration, in most cases, means copying the way of life of these celebrities (good or bad). It is therefore extremely important that we identify positive role models for our children that will help them shape their lives for the betterment of the society.

As a young man, I copied everything about Fela; as a new person in Christ, my admiration for Fela remains very high—without necessarily agreeing with all aspects of his lifestyle. But this book is not a judgement on Fela; he is mentioned because my story would not be complete without my "Fela years." He was my hero, and for many Nigerian people, he remains an inspiration, full of power, strength, and courage.

TWO-TIMING THE POLICE FORCE

For a while now, you could say I had been two-timing the police. I had been secretly assisting Fela instead of doing my official duty of hindering him. But now I was determined to avoid being a "zombie" altogether. If this was what the police force was, then I wanted no further part of it. My old problem returned: what to do with my life? Hearing that I wanted to leave the police, Fela had kindly offered me the chance to be a member of his band and be employed as a backing singer and musician. He had even said he would teach me how to play instruments. I couldn't play anything, but I could sing quite well and knew all his lyrics. I felt honored to be asked, but I had to turn it down. It would be all wrong, I told him, to be his employee. All I wanted was to be his friend, and that I would do for free.

My way out came quite by chance. I was heading home one day, off duty after the night shift, when I passed a man being harassed by two officers that I knew. His car had been pulled over, and they were searching it. One of the officers was pushing him around, crumpling his impeccably smart business suit. We had an odd/even license plate system in Lagos at the time. According to your number, you could only drive on certain days and at certain times. This was ostensibly to keep the volume of traffic at a manageable level, but really it just gave policemen a pretext to stop drivers and demand bribes. Not everyone could afford two cars—one to drive on each alternate day (which is how the richer people got round the rule)—and not everyone could keep track of the days. There would always be jobs to get to, errands to run, appointments to attend—the business of daily life. Inevitably somebody slipped up.

It was early morning, but it was still dark. It was easy to think that the nighttime rules still applied, but technically as soon as the clock struck six, the even-number day was in progress. In fact, it was only a few minutes past six, and the officers were already on the prowl, waiting for somebody to make a mistake. They could see that the man was obviously well off, and there was money to be made. Since there were two of them, the man would have no chance of being believed if he tried to alert the authorities. They were just about to haul him down to the police station. For some reason this angered me. I saw this kind of thing all the time, but today it just made me mad. I pulled over and got involved. As lower-ranked officers, they were forced to obey me when I told them to let the man go. They lost out on their bribe, much to their annoyance.

A few weeks later, I was driving to work at a similar time in the morning. I pulled up in the car park by the quayside in order to have my habitual breakfast of marijuana and local gin, which gave me the boost I needed to go and do my job. I wandered along by the water, enjoying the high, and letting the stress leave my body. Reluctantly I returned to my car and prepared for work, but just as I was getting into the driving seat, a man approached me across the car park. As he came closer, I saw it was the same man I had saved from extortion not so long ago. Dressed once again in an impossibly smart suit, he smiled and greeted me, thanking me for what I had done. He said he had immediately recognized my face, because it stood out as different from ordinary officers.

"You are too honest to be a policeman!" He exclaimed. "You're too nice. The police force is for corrupt people." He handed me his business card and invited me to his office for an interview. He worked in the HR department of one of the largest banks in Lagos. It was a tempting offer, and it was not long after attending the proposed interview that I took up the post of Banking Officer. At first this involved mostly cashier work at the front desk, but I quickly graduated to processing payments, debits (pin receipts) and checks.

The pay was better than the police force, but not anything impressive. When I tried to resign from the force, I had told my superior that I wanted to go on to further study rather than tell him the real reason for wanting to leave. He encouraged me to keep on as a policeman, as he said I had the potential to move up the ranks. Instead of leaving the force altogether, he suggested that I change to permanent night shift (a job nobody wanted). The night shift was a sort of joke—you could go out on patrol, drive around, smoke a bit, and go home. Nobody monitored you, so it was pretty easy to get away with working minimal hours (sometimes no hours) and still claim a full-time salary. He did not know that I had another job, thinking that I was going to the Technology College during the day—and I never told him, wanting to keep both salaries to fund my ever-growing drug expenses.

This went on for some months before anybody noticed. I was working on the cash desk at the bank one day, when one of my colleagues from the police force walked in to withdraw some money. As luck would have it, he came to my window.

"Inspector Lawrence? When did you start working here?" he asked, in a shocked voice. "When did you leave the police force? You never told me!" The queue was building up behind him, and my colleagues, who did not know about my double life, turned to stare.

"I just resigned," I lied. I would have to resign now.

So I stopped collecting my second salary, but never officially resigned—I just avoided the Lion Building from now on. My name was never actually taken off the payroll though, and according to my friends in the force, a mystery person kept collecting my salary for a long time after. I had become a "ghost worker," earning money for somebody else, joining the company of hundreds of expats or deceased people whose names are used falsely by some Nigerians desperate for more money. This was how, even after I stopped working for the Nigerian Police Force, my name still continued to cheat them of a salary. In the end, it turned out I was a corrupt official after all!

Chapter Six

DOWNWARD SPIRAL

I worked in various parts of the bank, familiarizing myself with the day-to-day procedures. It was a steady job, and I was grateful for the opportunity. The only problem was the salary. Now that I wasn't claiming my police wages, the money I earned at the bank was barely enough to keep my drug habit going, let alone pay for life's necessities.

In my quest to get hooked up with marijuana every week, I had met quite a few big players in the Lagos underworld. The more I saw of them, the more I started to wonder why they should get all the nice cars, jewelry, and clothes, while I should be slaving away every day with nothing to show for it. What I didn't think about was all the people they used and abused in order to get their wealth. It didn't seem to matter. Only what was visible mattered to me. My eyes were blinded by the glitz of their lifestyle.

My friend Vic used to pick me up from work just to show me how nice it was to drive home in a brand-new Mercedes Benz instead of my old Peugeot. Another friend, Ralph, used to invite me round just so I could be dazzled by the sheer amount of stuff he owned. His living room was out of this world, a gaudy shrine to consumerism. He had new suits in every color of the rainbow, enough to wear a different one every day of the year—but instead of keeping them in a wardrobe, he would hang them up in the living room on a rail going right round the walls. He had another rack for his shoes—"skin" shoes—all types of leather, all colors and styles, right across from one end of the room to the other. Despite not having a proper job, he was able to buy anything he wanted. Both he and Vic also had access to all the drugs they could possibly want, at any time. It did not take much for me to want to emulate them, but on my salary I could only dream of buying such expensive things.

They readily gave me some advice. The best way to get around the problem of a low salary was to start a "business" on the side. They knew some people who worked in my bank, and with their help we could all make quite a profit.

The plan was to start small, with frequent low-grade withdrawals, say N200 or N300. I got managers to sign PIN slips for me, allowing me to take money from an account that didn't necessarily have enough in it to cover the payment. The same went for checks. We would get a supply of checks straight from the mint, forge the amount and signature for a certain account, and then process them. When the fraudulent PIN slips and checks reached the clearing room, we would have a man on the inside—sometimes me—to intercept and destroy them. It was surprisingly easy. The slips just disappeared, so there was no way of tracing them. If the check didn't bounce (which it couldn't once we had removed it from the system), then the bank assumed that it was honored. Only one section of the bank had a computerized system, so all the paying in and withdrawing was done by hand—it was only the final accounts which were computerized. By the time the deficit reached the computing department and was discovered, the evidence had already vanished. The deficit was just written off as a mistake. The amounts were small enough not to worry a bank of that size.

We quickly got bolder and began to attempt even bigger withdrawals. After a few months we had stolen a million Nigerian naira (which in 1977 was a truly incredible amount). The naira was strong against the dollar at the time, making our bounty the equivalent of over a million dollars. The bank could not fail to notice the loss of these larger amounts, and they began to crack down on incompetence and simple mistakes, causing several innocent people to lose their jobs. It seemed like nobody could touch us—there was nothing to pin us to the crime, so we carried on as before.

My newfound wealth went to my head. I went crazy, buying new clothes, shoes, jewelry, gold wristwatches, and kilos of drugs. I bought two new cars (finally getting my own brand-new Mercedes), visited the most expensive nightclubs in Lagos, and hired prostitutes almost every night. I spent hundreds of naira on drinks, treating my friends and even paying for their own escorts and prostitutes. We often had weekends abroad too, flying out to Rome on a Friday night, watching football on Saturday, shopping in all the designer stores, and then getting a return flight to Lagos on Sunday. For such a hectic lifestyle, marijuana just wasn't enough anymore, so I began to drink increasingly large amounts of alcohol. Drinking heavily all weekend, I would stay on a permanent high, and then I could return to work on Monday with an enormous sense of well-being—the feeling of having had it all. Once again I was in my comfort zone, having everything on tap, whenever I wanted it.

The crash came sooner than expected. One of my friends at the bank had been watching my behavior carefully. Nobody could have failed to notice my sudden increase in spending, and he wanted to know where I got my extra cash. He said he wanted in on whatever little business venture I had going, often commenting while at my house that he would love to be able to afford nice clothes like me. As he was a friend, I shared with him the details of the gang's next move and told him that if he played his part correctly, he would go home with a cut of the profits. It was nice to have somebody to work with. The other guys involved in the fraud often cheated each other, wanting a bigger cut. They also ganged up on me, taking the majority of the cash for themselves. This meant I got a much smaller percentage than they did, in spite of me doing most of the work, and I was fed up of it. With my colleague on my side, I would be able to pull a job on my own and leave out the others.

I did what I always did: I made the transaction, and then waited for my colleague to remove the offending check. He came to me later on with the check for me to destroy. I opened the staff door to go outside, and suddenly plainclothes policemen surrounded me as if from nowhere. The bank had alerted the authorities, and they had appeared to arrest me on a charge of fraud. In panic I stuffed the check into my mouth and managed to chew it a little. This didn't stop them from getting hold of it, and they brought it to the station as evidence. I could not understand how I had been exposed. It was not until a witness statement was read against me that I realized what had happened. The denouncement had come from none other than my friendly colleague, the man I had trusted to assist me with the scam.

Apparently, in return for giving evidence against me, the bank would reward him with ten percent of the money that would have been lost, which worked out to several hundred thousand naira. This was less than he would have received for his part in the fraud, but it was an easier, legal reward. Every time he had come to my house he had simply been spying for the bank, gathering evidence to use against me. He told them about everything I bought, where I went, how much I spent, all the trips I took abroad, the company I kept—but however much he told them, it still remained that there was no concrete proof of my guilt. My lawyer played this card very strongly, but the entrapment story of my colleague was enough for the police. It seemed strange to me that the last time I had seen the inside of a cell was after I had testified against the government on behalf of

Fela—an unjust arrest. This time I deserved to be here. I could only hope that my lawyer was as good as he said he was.

Funnily enough, it was actually the manner in which my colleague had betrayed me that paved the way for my release. The police had replaced the original check with a fake, suspecting that I might try to destroy the evidence when I was arrested. I made reference to the serial number of this fake check in my police statement, and of course it did not correspond with the number of the check that was actually paid into the bank. The police had unwittingly shot themselves in the foot and had obliterated their own evidence. The entrapment had failed.

Acting on the word of my colleague, the bank had fired me immediately on the grounds of fraud. But as nothing had actually been proved due to the lack of evidence, and my case had not even gone to court, my lawyer pointed out that the bank was guilty of unfair dismissal, even slander. This was a serious charge for a large business with a good reputation to preserve, and they did not want to add to the already embarrassing failure to prevent fraud within the company. In exchange for my resignation, they agreed to drop all charges against me and settle out of court. It was a miracle that I did not end up serving a prison sentence. I did not even have to pay back any of the money, as they could not technically prove that I had stolen it, even though everybody at the bank knew by this time that I had been the one committing the fraud.

In the face of the huge loss sustained by the bank, the management decided to change regulations regarding cash withdrawals. Banks all over Nigeria began to take more precautions to prevent fraud and limit criminal activity. The cashier was now instructed to take a photograph of anybody wanting to withdraw over N5,000. This made it much more difficult for fraudsters to access accounts and made the police aware of anyone trying to withdraw large sums of money.

My colleague got a handsome reward for exposing my fraudulent activities. Not only did he get a large lump sum in cash, the bank also gave him a promotion and a transfer to the branch in Kaduna. Years later I heard rumors of the bank sponsoring an expensive London education as a continued reward for his loyalty and service. At first it enraged me that my friend could betray me like that, and that I had been fool enough to believe in his friendship, but I now realize that he had been doing the right thing, and that all the time he had been working in the interest of his employer. In his case, staying on the straight and narrow certainly had its rewards. In my case, greed for money and drugs killed any ambition I had to work at a career or do anything worthwhile. I had no patience to wait for a pay rise. I wanted everything now.

I had worked at the bank for less than a year. In that time I had gone from being a member of the prestigious Institute of Bankers in both Nigeria and London to narrowly escaping a long prison sentence. I had no references and no prospects. The man who had given me the job was disgusted with me and did not want to see my face again. I was truly sorry for paying him back in that manner. In spite of this, I was not prepared to give up any of my new possessions. In fact, I wanted even more. I had a hopeless drug addiction to feed. With no way of maintaining the life I was now used to, I had to find other ways of making money. Once again, the life of crime seemed to offer a quick fix.

LIVING ON CREDIT

I had to think of how to make money and quickly too. I got in with some people who were running credit card scams. You would offer to buy the owner's credit card along with their debt. It is amazing how many people fell for this. You had a few days, or even a week if you were lucky, to use the credit card as much as possible before the owner realized that he was still getting charged, and reported the card stolen. In that time, we would easily make back the paltry amount we paid for the card, plus a host of extras: nights in luxury hotels, plane tickets, designer clothing. Often you could buy an expensive piece of jewelry on credit, then sell it on immediately for half its value and still make a fortune. I made quite a good business out of selling first-class plane tickets at cut rates.

We could also make money by selling the credit card numbers on to people all over the world, who would then make replica cards and use them until the number was cancelled. On the side, I frequently travelled into the neighboring country of Benin to buy cheap shipments of contraband items which I then smuggled into Nigeria. Liquor was expensive, and there was a huge demand for black-market "hot drinks," especially whiskey. I would also buy large quantities of cheap textiles and fabrics for which there was a large market in Lagos.

This tided me over nicely for more than a year, after which my family intervened. In spite of the bank scandal, which had been splashed across all the papers, my uncle J.O. thought he would do me a favor and help me find another "proper" job. J.O. was Chief Accountant at one of the most renowned insurance companies in Lagos, and he recommended me to the manager to be included on the list of candidates for the company entrance examinations. I don't think he actually expected me to pass, because he was very surprised when I did! I also performed very well at the interview, and the company decided to take me on.

As soon as I started work, various relatives started dropping by the company to see if it was true that I had wormed my way into another cushy job. They would pretend to be visiting my uncle, but really they just wanted to confirm the rumors they had heard about my miraculous "comeback." Always putting on a smile when they saw me, once in the safety of my uncle's office, they would proceed to talk about me behind my back:

"J.O., I'm surprised at you. You mean you are not afraid to employ Solution in the accounts department, of all places?"

"Do you want Solution to send you to prison?"

"Don't you know he was sacked from the bank?"

To which he would calmly reply, "You people don't know Oji, but I know him." He knew my story, and what I had been accused of, but he also said he knew my true character—and given the chance, and the right opportunity, he believed I could be trusted.

They thought he was mad. "You're playing with fire," they warned him, going on to prophesy that I would ruin him, cause him to be sacked because of my dishonesty, or disgrace him with my bad behavior.

Aware of the massive amount of faith my uncle had in me, I tried hard to keep my head down. I actually enjoyed many aspects of the job, travelling all over the country to audit the accounts of various branches of the company, and I did very well. If I could have adapted to a normal salary, an honest wage, I could have made something of the opportunity, but before long the need for more money began to eat away at me once again. I just could not limit my spending. With absolutely no self-control, I would end up blowing my whole month's salary in a day. Since this wasn't the bank, I couldn't just take the cash. I needed to come up with a different sort of scam, one which was suited to the insurance business.

I arranged special deals with clients who I persuaded to insure with our company. For a small fee I would tell them how to legitimately submit a false claim on their insurance (sometimes as soon as three days after registering), mostly for motor vehicles insured with us, and I would make sure that the claim went through all the right channels. If policemen needed bribing to make a false statement supporting the claim, then I would sort that out, and I pushed the application through the claims process as quickly as possible using my inside influence. Eventually the client would be issued with a check payout, which I would get a small percentage of, but even with this extra money, I still did not have enough. The process was slow, and the amount I made was never quite worth the time and effort it took to arrange.

In order to supplement my salary with a regular large amount, I took to peddling marijuana in the city. It was easy to get hold of from other Nigerian towns, and I could drive to Bendel at the weekends to pick up grass at an extremely low price. I would then sell it at "bunks" (illegal liquor and drug dens) in Owerri, Aba, and Lagos, having several friends who ran these sort of joints. My colleagues were aware of my drinking, drug-taking, and all the late nights at clubs and brothels; they didn't say anything, but I could tell they didn't really want me there. My moods could be unpredictable; I smoked and sometimes drank before coming into work and often got high on my lunch break. The fact that I avoided doing anything illegal on the premises meant that they had no grounds to sack me (I'd fortunately stopped my trade in fraudulent claims before anyone found out), and I still did a reasonable job on the accounts. Then I did something which shocked them all.

I had been dating one of my colleagues for a while, a beautiful girl called Sarah. I had never been faithful to her, continuing to see other women regularly, and sleeping around with no respect for her feelings—but when it came to *her* faithfulness, then I had double standards. I arrogantly expected her to see only me, and in my hypocrisy I would not tolerate her being seen with other men or even speaking to them in my presence. I was jealous and possessive; the amount of marijuana I smoked only served to make me more paranoid.

One day an ex-boyfriend of Sarah's came to visit her in the office. He was staying as a guest with her family, and they were very close, having known each other a long time. It enraged me to see them talking together like old friends, and I vowed to teach her a bitter lesson. After work that evening I drove round to her house, parking just down the road. I could see her sitting outside the compound in the company of her sister and a few other relatives. Wanting to find out for myself what was going on, I took the spare key she had given me and crept round the back. Accessing her room, I found the boyfriend asleep on her bed, and hearing her happy laughter outside, I flew into a frenzy.

I marched outside and dragged her straight off the chair she was sitting on. Her relatives started shouting at me, but none of them dared to intervene. I hit her hard till even her cheekbones were bruised. My rage did not diminish until she lay on the floor, hard-pressed to move. Her sister was appalled and ran to her side, screaming at me to leave. I told Sarah that she'd better bring a spare dress to work tomorrow because I would surely rip it from her body and strip her naked for the whole office to see.

I didn't actually expect her to come to work the next day, but there she was. She had a large purple bruise under one eye, and her arms and legs were covered in dark marks. In her hand she carried a spare dress. Instead of realizing that the girl was terrified of me and had taken my ranting seriously, I thought she was trying to provoke me, winding me up and daring me to carry out my threat. Stupidly I thought that if I didn't make an exhibition of her, then she would lose respect for me, and I wanted to be sure that she would not cross me again.

In the cold light of day I did not have quite the same rage in me as I had had the previous evening, so I decided to recreate it. When break time came, I went out and bought a bottle of whisky. Downing that, combined with several potent spiffs, put me in the right mood. I was angry again, but being under the influence of drugs also made me feel that I was somehow not responsible for my actions. It almost made me think that what I did was excusable, but of course it was very deliberate, calculated.

When I returned to the office, most of my colleagues were out on lunch, but not all. Undeterred, I found Sarah at her desk, forced her backward, and ruined her dress with a pair of scissors. After I had finished, she quietly went and changed into the replacement she had brought with her that morning.

The horrified witnesses told their story to the rest of my colleagues, and the news quickly reached my uncle. He was so disappointed, he who had believed so strongly in me. He wanted to call the police and have me arrested for assault, but I managed to persuade Sarah to tell him that it was an accident, and that I had somehow caught and ripped her dress as I passed by on the way to my desk. It was a blatant lie, but if Sarah was not willing to press charges, then there was nothing the police could do. I was forced to leave the company. Nobody wanted me there. My attitude stank, and my behavior had become, quite frankly, alarming. I had no regard for anyone or anything, and I no longer cared about the job.

Sarah had mercy on me because she loved me and didn't want me to go to prison, but I did not deserve it. I will always regret the disgusting way I treated her. I was so selfish that I didn't care if I hurt her or not. She loved me, but I loved nothing but drugs.

Chapter Seven

MONEY TO BURN

My friends started to avoid me. Nobody wanted to accept a lift from me in case my car was searched and the police found drugs in the vehicle. And because I always carried drugs on me, nobody offered me a lift either. I began to associate mostly with drug dealers and other addicts. These friends encouraged me to try other drugs, and I began dabbling in heroin. At first I didn't like the experience. It made me feel horribly sick, and I did not enjoy the feeling, but, as with all hard drugs, it was highly addictive, and I quickly became hooked. Very soon after that I had my first encounter with crack, which was even more addictive. The dealer who introduced me to it was quite savvy. He knew that I had easy access to heroin. I now bought it regularly for my own personal use as well as selling it to make a bit of money. The street value of heroin was lower than that of crack, so he cleverly offered me a gram of crack in exchange for five or more grams of heroin. I would eagerly exchange heroin for my preferred drug, oblivious to the huge amount of money I was losing in the process. Money no longer meant anything to me, just a way of filling my crack pipe. It was literally going up in smoke.

I socialized in "bunks," and spent most of my time either getting high, or finding the money to get high. One dealer, popularly
known as "Where Your Own?" had his whole family working at
his "bunk." One of his wives would sell the drinks, and the other
would make hot pepper soup. He had a rule that you had to buy
something; otherwise, you couldn't stay, hence the nickname. If
you were bringing your own drugs to smoke, then you had to
purchase a drink or some soup. If you didn't want to eat or drink,
then you had to buy drugs. This way he ran a very profitable
business. Many of these bunk owners were my friends, as they
were the ones who supplied me with cannabis when I first
started dealing. I kept them as business contacts, but increasingly,
I would be entering their bunks in order to get high, rather than
to make any deals. My addiction quickly destroyed any business
sense I ever had.

Sometimes I would smoke constantly for days without sleeping or eating. When the drug had a hold on me, there really was
no time for anything else. It eclipsed the world. Once I sat in a
bunk smoking crack all day. When I came out, my eyes were
bloodshot, and I lolled drowsily against the wall, good for nothing. A young boy who was standing next to me looked at me in
disgust and said that if I were his older brother, he would never
talk to me again. Even a child could look at me and see that I
was a waste of space.

I can't remember having a girlfriend during that time, or any
meaningful relationships of any kind. The only women I knew
were in the drug trade, or fellow drug addicts. If they had no
money to get high, they would sleep with me in exchange for
drugs for themselves or even for their husbands. A lot of men
pimped out their girlfriends or wives so that they could have a fix.
I shudder to think how callous I was that I could take advantage
of women who were so vulnerable and desperate. Other women
would be traffickers, completely uninterested in relationships or
even sex, focused only on business. I would sometimes work with

them and share profits, but never have anything more. It was a world without love.

My addiction to crack was so total that it began to consume my income as well as my life. I should have remembered the drug dealer's mantra: "Don't get high on your own supply." Forgetting this, I slowly got into debt, unable to make enough money to feed my addiction. I was my own major client. My friends said the amount of money I spent on crack would have been enough to build an entire factory. I sold my clothes, my gold chains. I even used my Mercedes Benz as collateral with a drug dealer, and because I could not pay him back in time, I lost it. Gradually I ran out of possessions to pawn or sell.

Once I went to see my mother, ostensibly to see how she was doing, but actually I just needed some money. She didn't have any to give me, so I took some of her jewelry and sold it. I also took my younger sister's jewelry. On another occasion, I needed a fix so much that I snatched my mother's wallet out of her hands and ran away with it. In tears, she chased me down the street imploring me not to become a thief. She could never have caught up with me, but she ran anyway. In spite of my great craving for crack, my conscience somehow managed to show itself, and I felt terribly ashamed. I slowed down and turned back, returning the wallet to its rightful owner. Though I could not look her in the eyes, I begged her for forgiveness. But she was so saddened, frustrated, and agonized by the life I had chosen for myself that she looked at me that sunny morning and said, "It is better for me if you die, so I will weep once and know that you are dead, rather than to see you living and causing me pain and endless tears." My life was such a waste, yet I didn't care.

The family started to fragment. With the eldest son a drug addict, there was nobody to take responsibility and keep everyone together. My other brothers helped my parents as much as they could, but I should have been there to support them. Instead, I was wasting all my money on drugs and leaving them to struggle in poverty. When I had money, I would make sure I was well-clothed and driving a flashy car. When I needed more money, I would sell them again. All through this endless cycle, there was never any thought of sparing something for my parents or siblings.

GOING INTERNATIONAL

I had begun selling small quantities of heroin, but it was never quite enough to make a killing. The amount of money I needed to sustain my crack habit was enormous. Extra money could be made smuggling contraband from the Republic of Benin, which I had done before. A friend who worked as a customs official on the Nigerian border with Benin gave me a tip. The town of Cotonou was a good place to pick up drugs cheaply, and it was relatively easy to transport them from there into Nigeria. If you knew the right customs officer, then it was a walk in the park. The success or failure of smuggling drugs into Nigeria depended very much on who was on duty. My friend made sure I was successful.

This occupation saw me into the 1980s, and with the new decade came a more strategic approach to drug smuggling. Instead of continuing in this hand-to-mouth fashion, dabbling in the small time, I wanted to make it big. Benin provided the first step up, but it was soon time to look for more lucrative operations. Europe proved to be the answer. There was a huge demand for heroin and cocaine in Spain, and through a Nigerian contact in Madrid, I was able to plan my first European operation. With the increase of my ambition came increased risk, but this only fuelled my excitement. I had no respect for my life or the lives of others—I loved living on the edge.

In spite of the direction my life had taken, I still harbored the desire to learn. Drugs had provided the easy way to make money, but they had also prevented me from achieving anything. I genuinely wanted to further my education and forge a career, so I explored the possibility of studying Economics. I applied to several universities abroad, and seriously considered going to the U.S. to gain a degree, but once again drugs were the deciding factor. It seemed to be much more difficult for me to get a regular supply in America than elsewhere. I had many more reliable contacts in India, Europe, and North Africa. In the end, I chose India.

In this roundabout way, I became a student of Punjab University in Chandigarh. I enrolled in the department of Economics and Public Administration, thinking that I could gain the skills to enable me to pursue a career in finance or something related. I continued to take drugs, but I also studied diligently, taking my studies seriously. On the side I peddled drugs, and my business grew steadily. Over the years I had built up a large network of contacts—dealers, clients and smugglers—many of whom were in India. Clients would fly over from Nigeria to be hooked up with a supply of heroin. They would wait in their hotel for me to arrive with the goods, and my excellent contacts meant that they never had to wait long. I always provided the best quality in the shortest time, and my clients were always satisfied.

I met a man called Alhaji, a Nigerian businessman, who used to come and smoke crack with us. Often he brought his Indian girlfriend with him. I never used to pay much attention to her even though she had hinted on several occasions that she would like us to date, until one day I found out that her family had a longstanding history of producing high-grade heroin. Suddenly she seemed very appealing, and I decided to succumb to her advances. She eventually became my girlfriend and left Alhaji, who at that time pretended not to mind. This way I was able to have a steady supply of heroin, even on public holidays (which India had more of, it seemed, than any other country of my experience!), when it was nearly impossible to do business. I was always sure of having clients as I would have the goods any day of the year.

My drug business became top priority, as I quickly grew used to the trade in India and had an amazing run of luck. To make sure that my luck continued, I joined a "cult"—one of the most feared in Nigeria—which had branches in several other countries. I was able to go regularly, whether at home or abroad, and this became my safeguard. I had become quite paranoid about my safety and the safety of my money. Now that I began to have regular large income, I wanted to preserve it. I had all sorts of talismans, charms, and rings that I believed to have magical powers of protection. I kept a gun with me all the time, especially when I was at home in the evening. You never knew when somebody would decide to stab you in the back, literally or metaphorically.

I could not trust anyone. Nevertheless, it seemed that the people I could trust the most were my own countrymen, so I surrounded myself with a small team of fellow Nigerians. They were also students at various universities, and with their help, I was able to take larger consignments back to Nigeria ready for their onward journey to Europe. A Nigerian flying directly to Spain or Italy from India was considered to be extremely suspicious, and your luggage was almost certain to be searched at the airport. To avoid the customs police, we would fly the drugs into Lagos, and then from Lagos to Madrid or Rome. It was still risky—especially with the military crackdown in Nigeria—but the drugs were more likely to make it to their destination undetected. I had been making small drug runs to Madrid for some time now, so I had all the contacts in place. The challenge was increasing the size of the consignments.

In 1984, after the military coup in Nigeria, the new military government headed by General Buhari introduced capital punishment for anyone convicted of dealing, selling, or taking cocaine or "similar drugs." They thought that this would reduce the amount of drugs trafficked in and through Nigeria, but it only made drug dealers think of more ingenious ways to smuggle them. The new laws passed by this military government should have posed some sort of deterrent to me. They didn't. It goes some way toward illustrating my recklessness to say that the prospect of a death sentence did not faze me. In fact, the very day that three well-known drug dealers were executed by firing squad in Lagos, I was booked on the midnight flight to Madrid with a kilo of cocaine strapped to my back in small packets. Other smugglers were freaked out by the implementation of the new laws and cancelled their trips, but I just didn't care. I actually enjoyed taking the risk. It made me feel alive.

Every time a route became "hot," or a certain method was exposed, I would change my tactics. It required you to think on your feet and be prepared to change plans at a moment's notice. If a particular airport had a crackdown, introducing cavity searches or x-rays, then I would transfer my booking to a different airline. If a particular country started to target Nigerian nationals for searches, I would use a fake passport. I had dozens of passports, some from different countries in Africa, some from South America, and some from the Caribbean or West Indies. Sometimes it would be necessary to fly to Brazil to pick up a consignment (cocaine from Bolivia), but most of the time, I was able to pick up the goods in India. The heroin came from Afghanistan via Pakistan. Sometimes I would need to go there, but generally I had enough contacts in India to allow me to avoid trips like that. My main task was getting the heroin out of Bombay and into Europe.

I had to be very inventive. Sometimes I would carry the drugs on my person, either in my clothes or in my hand luggage. I had many different suits to take on each trip, and each one would have a small quantity of heroin or cocaine sewn into the lining. The suits would then be packed in my suitcase along with a thermos flask or a hot plate which would have drugs inserted into the vacuum alongside the metal lining. Occasionally I would have the packets taped directly onto my skin under my clothes. Before x-ray machines were introduced into airport security measures, this was very easy to do, but soon it became much more of a risk to put anything in your luggage. It became standard practice to swallow the majority of your consignment, usually in ten gram ovules made from balloons or condoms, although this method of transportation carried a different risk. Other times I would use a technique known as "boxing," where you claimed to be importing something—say, a kitchen appliance—but in each box a small amount of drugs would be hidden amidst the packaging.

THE RICH NIGERIAN STUDENT

I was away so often it's a wonder I got any college work done, but I did manage to keep up with my studies. I got quite involved in university life and joined a fraternity called the Pirates, comprised of Nigerian expats studying at the university. We wanted to have our members installed as student representatives and so have control over student affairs, influencing how college money was spent and how the university was run. It was so important to us that we decided to try to disrupt the elections for the Nigerian Society, as we knew that none of the other students would vote for our candidates. We thought that by secretly destroying the ballot boxes we could claim that somebody else had been attempting to rig the voting, and so increase our chances next time by discrediting the opposition.

Election day was so heated that Indian policemen were dispatched to the voting hall in order to maintain law and order. To gain access to the hall, I posed as a Nigerian policeman. I still had my ID card from my police days in Nigeria, as well as some photographs of me in uniform, and I pretended that the government had sent me to supervise the elections on behalf of the huge number of Nigerian students currently studying at Punjab University. Amazingly they believed me and let me into the hall where the ballot boxes were. The plan was to disable the lights and allow the other Pirates to seize the boxes. I managed the first part, and the hall was plunged into darkness. The others moved into position, but we hadn't counted on the fierce resistance of the ballot officers. Whenever we tried to get hold of a box, the officer would shield it with his body and ward off the attack.

We ended up with nothing, and before the lights went back on, we hadn't even managed to damage a single box, let alone get hold of them. Fortunately we got away before anyone saw us, and the police never found out that I was involved in the disturbance. I dread to think what sort of punishment I would have got for impersonating a police officer.

Keeping those police pictures was a good idea though. They saved my skin several times. I was living in Chandigarh, close to the university campus, in an apartment with a fellow Igbo. This friend was special to me because of our shared heritage, and I treated him like a brother, lending him money and giving him drugs whenever he needed them. One day I decided to deny him any more credit, as he owed me a very large amount of money and didn't show any signs of trying to pay it back. I still gave him drugs to sell on the street so that he could make a bit of money, and I let him live in the apartment for free, but I thought it was reasonable to curb his spending. He was angry and decided to get back at me. As soon as I went out to do some shopping, he phoned the police and tipped them off about the large stash of drugs that I had hidden in the apartment.

The neighbors told me afterward that the police arrived and rushed inside, demanding to see me. My roommate told them that I would be back any minute, so they could go ahead and search the apartment. Just then, the inspector on duty caught sight of my police photos which I had framed and hanging on the wall. He asked my roommate who the man in the pictures was, and he told them.

"But I know this man!" The inspector exclaimed. He told his boys that he knew me to be a good man, an ex-policeman no less, who used to live near him in Sector 15, and he had no idea that I had moved recently to Sector 38. Because he knew and respected me, he asked his boys to call off the search and leave my apartment alone. I was spared arrest that day because of my old uniform, and my friend's plan was foiled.

I got home to find my room in a mess, the wardrobe doors broken off, and the money I had kept inside gone. My friend told me that it was the police who had ransacked the place, and I had no reason to disbelieve him. I only found out later that the police had not touched a thing, and that it was my friend who had stolen my money. The fact that he moved out almost immediately after that and was suddenly able to afford to rent his own place should have raised my suspicions, but someone who had my trust could abuse it for a long time before I turned against them.

I often helped people out. I was very kind and generous... sometimes foolishly so. At the time, I thought nothing of giving away my last money if I perceived the person needed it more than I did. I would give away large quantities of drugs free to people—most times to the surprise and consternation of such people. Interestingly, people began to call me "Solution." People generally believed that, once they brought their problems to me—financial or otherwise—I would do my utmost to provide them with a solution. And this was very true as I normally would stop at nothing to make sure I helped people in need, whether genuine or fake—because there were certainly people who capitalized on my generous nature and came with fake problems just to con me out of my money. My Indian landlord came to me one day in a state because a Nigerian tenant in one of the rooms downstairs had died suddenly of a heart attack due to overwork. The landlord could not find anyone to fill the room, and he was losing rent. The Nigerians refused to live in a room where somebody had died, as it had a bad spirit in it, and none of the Indians wanted to live in a crack den. I tried unsuccessfully to persuade some students to take the room, so in the end I agreed to take it over myself. Even though I didn't need to rent two floors of a building, I decided to help him out. The downside of having so much unnecessary space was that it attracted freeloaders, and I ended up letting many people stay with me for nothing.

I gave away drugs, and I gave away money. I paid school fees, found people housing, gave people business start-up loans, and looked after the families of friends when they were short of money. People came to me if they needed anything. People even came to me when they *didn't* need anything and were just pretending to be in need. The reputation of being indiscriminately generous meant that I was also gullible and easily conned. I treated everyone the same. Everyone, that is, except my own family.

Whenever I was in Lagos, I would stay in the best hotels, eat at the best restaurants, and drive around in the best cars. I would give away money to whoever needed it, but during all these visits I never thought about visiting my family or sending any money home. Inevitably people would bump into someone from my family and thank them for the help I had given them, saying that they must be proud to have such a generous relative—but the family member would know absolutely nothing about it. My family never saw this generous side of my nature. I avoided doing my duty and instead squandered my money on people I thought were friends. If only I had known that the type of people I considered friends back then were only using me, perhaps I would have given my attention to people who deserved and most needed it.

My family was living in poverty. It was quite an insult to them to hear reports of me squandering my money on meaningless luxuries when they had barely enough to eat. I was a source of pain and humiliation to them. My grandmother had a scathing nickname for me: "Omezie onye akwuna, nne ya gba oto," meaning, "he who clothes a prostitute while his own mother is going around naked."

When strangers stole from me or double-crossed me, I would often just walk away but not so with members of my family. My cousin William—an underpaid immigration officer—once succumbed to the temptation of tampering with my stash when he gave me a lift to the airport. I was flying to Madrid, and it was not until I arrived that I noticed I was missing over two hundred grams of heroin. When I returned to Lagos, a dealer told me that William had been trying to sell the heroin to him during my absence. I was so angry that I stormed round to William's house, confronting him aggressively; then, when it was clear that he could not pay me back, I seized his car as compensation. The money from selling the car did not equal the amount of money I had lost from that heroin sale, but it made me feel better to know that I had done something.

As soon as my family heard of this, they pleaded with me to return the car, saying that whatever wrong William had done, it didn't entitle me to take his vehicle. Little did they know I had already sold it. To get some peace, I later sent my uncle the exact amount of money I had got from the sale of the car. It was a small amount, as the car had been an old one and not worth very much. This money could not have bought William a new car, but I considered it to be discharging any obligation to my family. Needless to say, they were not impressed.

ALHAJI'S REVENGE

I was oblivious to everything except my own pleasure. My luck was so extraordinary that I believed myself to be immune to danger. But whatever enemies I had in the drug world, and whatever threat the authorities posed, was nothing compared to the danger I posed to myself. I was my own worst enemy. My out-of-control drug-taking proved to be a problem, not just because of the health risks it carried, but also because of the effect it had on my business acumen. On one occasion I was due to fly to Madrid on a Tuesday evening with a consignment. I checked into my hotel in Colaba, Bombay, on the Monday night and started smoking. I smoked such a quantity of heroin that I fell into a stupor. When I awoke I was very cold—the withdrawal effects of the heroin had begun to kick in—and I realized that I had been there for several days. I had missed my flight and screwed up my business deal.

It was not only business which was jeopardized by my drug addiction. My university work suffered too. It may seem strange to think that a professional drug-dealer could be concerned about getting a degree, but I made sure that I kept up with my studying. Most of the time I attended my classes and turned in all my assignments, but when I went on a spree, my diligence went out of the window. Sometimes I would smoke for an entire week without leaving my room. During these sprees I would not sleep, the cocaine keeping me wide awake and the heroin bringing me down again, floating me up and down on an endless sea of highs. Nothing else entered my mind—the drugs had complete hold over me.

Consequently, I forgot important dates, missed appointments, and even missed some university exams. Generally my work passed muster, and so the struggle to balance my education and drug business continued, even though the importance of getting a degree seemed irrelevant now that my drug-dealing business had reached such proportions. Not surprisingly, I had made quite a reputation for myself—"the rich Nigerian student who was fearless, kind, and generous to a fault." Little did I know that all the wealth I had managed to accumulate would come crashing and that the first year after university would be such a trying one.

My friend Alhaji, the Nigerian businessman, had never quite forgiven me for 'stealing' his girlfriend. He never mentioned it, but it was always there, hanging over our friendship. We continued to associate and smoke together, and I always supplied him with drugs whenever he was in India on business. But while I had forgotten about it, he was still inwardly seething. To be honest, I thought that everything was fine. I didn't place that much importance on girlfriends, so it didn't cross my mind that he might still be angry with me.

One night he accompanied me to a meeting where I purchased a heroin consignment I was planning to take back to Nigeria with me the next day. He was going to fly with me to Lagos and carry some of the weight, so afterward we went back to my place with the drugs to have a smoke. We took a taxi back to my apartment, and we sat chatting side by side in the back. When we got home, I realized that my passport and ticket were missing. I had kept them close to me all day in my suit jacket pocket to make sure that I did not lose them, and I couldn't understand how they had suddenly disappeared. Alhaji helped me to search the apartment and the street outside, but of course we couldn't find them. If they were still in the taxi, my chances of getting them back were next to zero.

The drugs had been packed by professional packers and were ready to go. I could not travel without my passport, so I had to entrust the entire consignment to Alhaji, who promised to get it to Lagos safely and bring me the proceeds on his next business trip. I was not too worried because he came to India very regularly. Meanwhile I would have to set about applying for a new passport, which for a Nigerian stranded in India was not an easy task.

It was a few months before I had any news of Alhaji. The story reached me through a fellow drug dealer who had just arrived from Lagos. The drugs had been sold by Alhaji as planned, but instead of returning to Bombay with my money, he had pocketed the proceeds. I was shocked to discover that he had no intention of coming back. This, then, was his revenge. He had planned it well. I realized that he must have taken my passport while we were sitting in the taxi, and then pretended to look for it when we got home, even though he knew very well what had happened to it. Because I had trusted him, I had not thought twice about letting him take the consignment to Lagos. My lack of awareness resulted in being double-crossed. I should have learnt my lesson by now, but for some reason I continued to trust people who clearly were not to be trusted. Even though I was addicted to drugs, I took friendship seriously and would never think of double-crossing any of my friends in a business deal.

For the first time, I took a good look at my life. I hated my lifestyle and the person I had become. I was constantly surrounded by people, yet I was so lonely. I bought brand-new cars only to end up exchanging them for some grams of crack cocaine whenever I ran out of drugs or cash to purchase drugs. False friends made sure they hung around me so that they would be the ones to buy off whatever valuables I was ready to part with at any given time to buy drugs—from Cartier wristwatches to gold rings and chains, I was a constant prey. Yet the same people who bought the valuables off me were there to consume the drugs free of charge with me. They saw me as a stupid person despite the fact that they lived off me. I wore the best of suits yet would sometimes sleep in uncompleted buildings; I made so much money without keeping any of it. What a miserable existence! I felt trapped…caged! I tried everything I could but still wasn't able to free myself.

Following Alhaji's betrayal, I was trapped inside India. It took me nearly a year to get a new passport and scrape enough money together to get myself out. Alhaji's betrayal had hit me hard. I began to smoke even more, and my money soon ran out without my international income. I had to return to touting and scouting: supplying African (particularly Nigerian) dealers with the goods for their consignments, or sometimes simply selling drugs to tourists. It was a big step down from what I had been used to. Once again my life hit a low patch, and the feeling of emptiness fuelled my drug habit—it was the only thing I had to fill the void. All through this time I had only one prayer on my lips: "Oh God, may I never run out of money such that I would not be able to buy drugs." To me this would have been a fate worse than death as I couldn't imagine living without drugs and I was too proud to beg.

Chapter Eight

FACING THE AWFUL TRUTH

After I got my new travel documents, I got straight back to business. I based myself in Bombay for drug runs, as the airport provided access to many different routes into Nigeria if the direct route was hot. Sometimes I would fly via Ethiopia, sometimes via Kenya. Occasionally it was necessary to go through Italy or another European country. I made several runs a month using different passports, so if immigration ever did suspect me, they could find no record of my previous trips. If I made a transit in Rome, I would swap my passport after checking in to my onward flight. I had my own immigration stamp, so with just a little ink and a different passenger name, I could make it look like I had been staying in Italy for a week rather than passing through on my way back from India. Visits to India, especially short ones (a day or two), were pretty much a giveaway to customs that you had only been there to pick up drugs.

I was in Lagos for a good part of each month, and I spent a good part of each month avoiding my family. Whenever they heard I was in town, somebody would try to get in touch with me, but I ignored them or pretended I had not got their messages. The most persistent was my younger brother Samuel. I had promised to help him out with his radio station. He needed a small amount of money (only 10,000 naira) to buy a more powerful transmitter so that he could broadcast to the whole state rather than just be limited to a small section of the city of Aba. I had made my promise, offhand, about a year previously, and I had reiterated it several times. He had been waiting ever since for me to keep my word. It was such a small amount to me—I would often spend ten times that amount on crack in a single day. He knew that I was not putting the money to any good use, that I was literally smoking it away. One day he lost his patience and came to look for me in Lagos.

He got the night bus from Aba, an uncomfortable journey which took about eight hours, and on his arrival tracked me down to an expensive hotel in the downtown area. He managed to get the clerk to give him my room number as he said he wanted to see his brother on an urgent matter. I was very surprised to see him there and was reminded of how much this new transmitter would mean to him. I assured him that I would help him, made some phony excuse as to why I hadn't kept my promise, and told him that because I didn't have any cash on me right now, he should keep a hundred grams of heroin from my stash, as that would provide the money he needed when it was sold. He had no idea where to sell the stuff, so I assured him that I would find a buyer—but that he should hang onto it for now to stop me smoking it. I must add that at the time, I really meant to let him have the money.

I disappeared with some friends, leaving him in the hotel room. He thought I was going to sort out a buyer for him, but I just wanted to get high. We went to another room that I had paid for in the hotel, and I exchanged my supply of heroin for the cocaine that my friends had with them. We smoked all day and deep into the night, until I had run out of heroin. It then occurred to me that I had some more back in the room where Sam was currently sleeping.

It was about four in the morning. I burst into the room and woke Sam up, telling him in an urgent voice that he needed to give me the drugs because I had heard that the police were about to raid the hotel. Sam looked at me skeptically and said he thought I was up to something. I persisted, telling him that he would get into a lot of trouble if the police found drugs in the room where he was staying.

"You don't think I checked in under my own name…" I said. He began to look worried, and in the end he gave me the packet of heroin. I told him to go back to sleep; I would go out and sell the drugs immediately to the buyer I had lined up, and then there would be nothing to worry about. I would be back in the morning with the money.

My brother went back to sleep, and the next morning he waited in the room for me. By midday, members of the hotel staff were banging on the door. They told him that if he didn't vacate the room immediately then he would be charged for another night. He asked where I was, but of course they had never heard of me. There was no way he could afford to stay in a five-star hotel, so he was forced to leave without seeing me. He was so frustrated and disappointed that he was in tears.

Meanwhile I had used the heroin to get more cocaine; I had inhaled Sam's transmitter money to gain a transitory high. I didn't give my brother a second thought, and I am ashamed to say that I didn't feel any remorse. All I wanted was my drugs, and nothing would stand in the way of me getting a fix. It was all the more terrible because of my fickle attitude to giving—I had no problems giving huge sums of money to complete strangers, but I found it impossible to give to my own family. In fact, a few days before my encounter with Sam, I had given triple this amount of money to a Spanish student who could not afford his plane ticket back to Madrid. It made no sense for me to treat a stranger as a brother but neglect my blood relatives. It still fills me with shame when I think about how badly I treated Samuel.

Where drugs were concerned, I had a complete lack of proportion. I was involved for a while with a ring of drug dealers in Bombay, some of them just small-time crooks in it for the heroin supply. We were celebrating a successful deal. One man suddenly fell ill; he had overdosed, and I went with him to the hospital. The doctors said he was in a very bad state, and that he might not live through the night. It was decided that I would stay with him until morning, when another friend would take over—that way the poor man would have somebody by his side all the time and would not be afraid. Late that night I began to get the urge to smoke, but I found that I was out of cash. I started searching his clothes which were laid out next to the bed. In his jacket pocket I found some money—his share of the profits from our recent deal.

"Solution," he said, seeing me take the money. "That money belongs to me."

"I know," I replied simply.

I wanted the drugs so badly that I didn't feel the need to justify myself. Not able to wait any longer I left him and went to score some crack. I spent the night getting high in a hotel. The next morning I returned to the hospital to find that he had passed away. I was deeply saddened that I had not been with him when he died, but I did not connect that failure with my own selfishness. It is tragic that I could place the importance of drugs above that of human life. My priorities were by now so horribly screwed up that I had no sense of right and wrong.

TRYING MY LUCK

I took many unnecessary risks during my drug runs. The trips were planned carefully, but I would always push my luck by carrying drugs on my person, or even smoking in public. It was as if I wanted to increase the danger I was in—it made my life seem so much more exciting. On one occasion, I even smoked on the plane. I had decided to fly via Kenya this time, and for some reason I was feeling reckless. I smoked crack right there in my seat. The whole aircraft reeked of drugs, and the flight attendants went and complained to the pilot that someone was jeopardizing the safety of the other passengers. He came and spoke to me himself, threatening to hand me over to the immigration police as soon as we landed. It seemed as though my luck had finally run out.

When we landed in Lagos, I was expecting to be greeted by a whole cavalry of customs officers. The door swung open, and I saw them, lined up against the wall of the exit tunnel. My eye caught that of the pilot, and I toyed briefly with the idea of begging him not to turn me in, but I realized that if he was going to turn me in he would already have done so, via radio. That's probably why they were all there: they were waiting for me. I took a deep breath and went toward them. It was like walking slowly towards hell, visions of beatings and torture and eventual death by firing squad.

To my surprise, none of them took any notice of me. The pilot made no move to report me to the officials, and nobody stopped me. I waltzed right through immigration, collected my bags, and was out of the airport before I had even had time to calm down. Nobody searched my things, and I had no questions asked of me at customs. It was probably the easiest and quickest exit I've ever had from an airport!

There were countless other narrow escapes. So many times my bags were searched, and the police or customs officials did not manage to find the drugs hidden in them—the professional packers had done their job well. It took someone with a special nose for the job—a second sense almost—to be able to spot the hiding places. There was a particular customs officer called Mama Calabar who instilled so much fear into people that many dealers would actually cancel their flights if they heard she was on duty. Another senior officer, from northern Nigeria, was reputed to have supernatural powers of detection. I landed one evening in Lagos after a flight from Bombay and was waiting by the carousels for my luggage. This terrifying man spotted me from a mile off and homed in.

Immediately, he called two more officers to his side and commanded them to search me as soon as I had retrieved my luggage. The drugs were sewn carefully into the lining of my suits, and I could only hope that they would not be able to find them. I counted on them being less experienced than this senior customs wizard. They went through my bags over and over again, but they did not turn anything up. The senior official was furious.

"Don't tell me what I know!" he shouted in sheer frustration. He looked at me, and I knew that he knew I had a stash. He just didn't know where. And I was not about to tell him.

Two more officers were called. We had quite a party now, and it was attracting attention. I was very embarrassed to be singled out in front of everyone in the airport. Fortunately, when the boss man ordered a "special search," he had the decency to have me taken to a private room. On the way there, I racked my brains. They had not found the stash in my luggage, but what would they do when they found the twenty grams of heroin reserved for personal use, tucked inside my pocket handkerchief?

We were nearing the office. I had to do something fast. Somehow I managed to maneuver the packet from my pocket and into my hand, and from my hand to the waistband of my trousers. I pushed the packet down into my trouser leg, and as it slid down I succeeded in kicking it behind one of the doors that we passed en route. I was just in time. When we entered the office, the first thing they took from me was my handkerchief. I was subjected to a thorough and intimate search, but of course they found nothing. The men then tried to intimidate me, trying to make me confess to where the drugs were hidden. Everyone believed I had drugs in my possession: their boss was never wrong. They even tried to make a deal with me, saying that they would help me avoid the death sentence if I only told them where the stash was. I laughed at them. Now that I had got rid of the evidence, I was confident again. They detained me for hours, but they could not make me confess, and in the end they had to let me go. I walked out of the airport feeling like a miracle had happened. My luck was simply astonishing.

There were warning signs, though. If the danger of the drugs themselves was not enough, coupled with the number of times I had almost been caught, then I should have paid attention to the uncanny supernatural signs which came my way. In 1989, I twice had very clear warnings from my grandmother. Once when I was high, I had an audio hallucination, hearing my grandmother's voice loudly telling me, "Lawrence, go home. Your mother is weeping for you."

Another time I was smoking with some friends, and suddenly one of them woke up out of the drug stupor they were in, and said almost exactly the same thing: "Solution, go home. Your mother is crying because of you." The worst thing was that I knew those words were true. I was breaking my mother's heart, but I couldn't care less.

LIVING HELL

At the end of 1989, something happened which should have made me rethink things. I lost everything, including my dignity, but somehow I still clung tenuously to life. My normal drug run had become overly complicated. Many people convicted for drug-related offences in Nigeria had told journalists that I was the one who introduced them to heroin and cocaine. I was notorious. My infamy unnerved me, and I was now afraid to land directly in Lagos with my consignment as I had been informed that police and customs officials were on the watch for me at the airport. The alternative—a long and ridiculously convoluted route—was travelling with Cameroun Airlines, transiting in the capital Duala where I would have a four-day layover, followed by a flight to Benin, and then a journey across the border to Lagos by road. I was faced with the biggest challenge of my life: how to survive for six days with a kilo of heroin in my stomach.

The flight to Cameroun from Bombay was uneventful. I got off the plane and entered the airport without being stopped; the other half of the consignment stashed in my luggage went undetected. Then I sat down to wait. I had to keep a low profile, as the airport police patrolled regularly for suspicious passengers and loiterers. Going into town to find a hotel would have created more problems—I wanted to avoid going anywhere near immigration and customs. To prevent any withdrawal symptoms giving the game away, I had to keep myself dosed up regularly, and so I made daily trips to the toilets where I would stay inside a cubicle for some time, sorting myself out. I forced myself not to eat anything even though I was starving, but despite my efforts I found it was impossible to hang around for four days without needing to use the facilities. After a while I began to pass out the little ovules of heroin that I had ingested. Every time one came out, I had to grit my teeth and swallow it again. I couldn't leave the cubicle at the risk of being spotted, so I used a bottle of Coca Cola to wash the packages as best I could, but nothing could mask the horrendous smell and taste. Exhausted and sick, all I could do was hope that I made it out of this living hell.

Day three dragged on, and I was running out of energy. I took the risk of leaving the airport building to get some fresh air. Almost immediately, I was approached by officers from the police patrol van stationed outside. Some of the men had seen me inside the airport several times over the last couple of days, and they wanted to know why I was in transit for so long. I made up some story about missing a connection and having to wait for the next available flight. I tried to act as though it was all a big inconvenience to me (and really, I didn't have to act very hard), telling them that my mother would be furious when I finally got home as I had missed an important family event. With baited breath, I awaited their reaction. If they didn't believe me, they would search me, and then the game would be up. It was a tense few minutes, but eventually they let me go, telling me that if they caught me wandering outside the terminal again they would have to arrest me for loitering.

I steeled myself for the final day. Coca Cola kept my blood sugars up, but I still felt weak and nauseated from lack of food. The flight to Benin fortunately ran as scheduled, and I began to relax a little, thinking that I had almost made it. I had another hit at the airport to boost my spirits. There was not long to go now, and when I hailed a cab, I thought it would be just over an hour before we had crossed the Seme border and neared Lagos. I was naïve to be so complacent. My time in the airport was practically risk-free in comparison to the road journey. For the whole duration of the taxi ride I was on the edge of my seat. At every kilometer we would encounter a government checkpoint. Police would demand money from the driver and the occupants of the car, ask to see documents, and conduct random searches of luggage. Although one kilo of the stash was well hidden inside my own body, the other three kilos would undoubtedly be found if anyone troubled to search my suitcase thoroughly. Luckily for me, the death penalty for convicted drug smugglers had just been abolished, but there was still a hefty prison sentence (often life imprisonment) for anyone caught trafficking or selling cocaine or heroin. And sometimes just being in police custody could be worse than prison itself.

Most checkpoints were negotiated with a small bribe, but one of them stopped the car and ordered a complete search of the vehicle. I had to feign nonchalance, as you could never be sure if the driver was in the employ of the government, and I said to him that I would just get out and smoke a cigarette while the men went over the car. They had the mats out, the boot open, pulled up the seats, looked in the glove compartment, inside the radio—and then they turned their attention to my luggage. My heart nearly stopped. It was all over. Surely they would find the packages in the suitcase. Although at the bottom, they would be instantly visible when the case was emptied. The man began rifling through my clothes; he pulled out a tie that he liked the look of, examined the pockets of a suit jacket, and then, inexplicably, threw the clothes back and closed the lid.

"OK, go," he waved his hand and walked back to the checkpoint.

I had to pretend that I was fine, that my heart was not beating wildly and that I was not having trouble breathing. I sighed deeply to get my breath, and the driver fortunately thought I was sighing out of boredom. The journey which should have taken an hour, had taken us six.

Once we arrived in Lagos, we instantly hit traffic. The jams were terrible downtown, and we sat there for half an hour without moving. I was itching to get into town and meet my friends to deliver the consignment. I decided to get out and walk down, leaving my stuff to wait in the taxi. The ovules were ready to come out, and I couldn't wait any longer. My friends were happy to see me, and I was greeted with shouts of "Baba Solution!"—the arrival of a fresh consignment was always celebrated. We had drinks and got high together. I quickly lost all track of time. We had had several hits of heroin before I thought about going to get my luggage. I went back to the main street to pay the taxi driver. In the meantime the traffic jam had dispersed, and everything was running normally. There was not a taxi in sight.

Frantically I ran up and down the street, searching all the side streets as well, but the taxi had disappeared. And with it had gone my entire luggage: my passports, my money, my clothes, and three kilos of high-grade heroin. I had lost everything I had risked my life for. After the nightmare of the journey, nearly a week of travelling in extreme discomfort and indignity, after much fear and sleeplessness and starvation, it had come in the end to nothing. I had nothing but my own stupidity to blame. My rush to get high had impaired my judgment, and I had made a very expensive mistake. I still don't know what happened to that taxi. Of course, my luggage was never recovered. Somebody must have had a field day.

All I had left were the ovules I had swallowed. In desperation, I went to see my cousin Stanley, who said he knew somebody who could get a buyer for me. I needed to sell them quickly so that I could at least make enough money to get back to India. The longer I waited, the more I would use to fuel my own habit, and the less I would have to sell. To help me out, Stanley paid for me to check into hospital to get some rehab treatment, but whatever they tried to do there had no effect on me. Stanley even arranged for me to be put in the local jail, thinking that if I was locked up and kept away from drugs, then I could not be tempted to use my stash. But after a whole month in a cell I came out and went straight back to heroin. It seemed impossible for me to live without drugs. They formed the whole purpose of my life. I had nothing else in the world that was important to me. Very quickly, the little supply I had left dwindled to nothing. I was stranded.

Not surprisingly, Lagos suddenly became a very unfriendly place. All the friends I had made in the drug world vanished from my life. My source of income had completely dried up. Now that I had no money to lend or give away, all the people who used to sponge off me conveniently forgot my existence. If they saw me in the street they would look the other way, pretending that they did not know me. From being a rich dealer I had sunk to the level of a poor junkie almost overnight. I realized that I had no real friends. Nobody really cared whether I lived or died. They only wanted me around if they knew they could get something out of me. Finally it dawned on me that my life was slowly wasting away: I had no career, no family, no genuine friends, no wife, and no children.

The only people I could turn to now were my family. And so the firstborn son crawled back east in shame.

I journeyed to Aba, where my younger brother Sam was living. I had no money, and only the clothes I stood up in, so I had to rely on his charity. In spite of the shabby way I had treated him years earlier, he was kind to me. A pastor cousin, Nick, saw my spiritual poverty, and gave me a Bible in the hope that I would be able to see that my problem was not physical, but spiritual. It was a beautiful Bible, leather-bound and smart. He had obviously spent a considerable amount on it and considered it to be a lifelong present. I didn't even open the packaging to take a look inside. As soon as he had left, I went out to find somebody who would give me money for it. In the circles I frequented, a Bible was not worth very much—in spite of the expensive binding and the gold lettering on the cover, I didn't get more than the equivalent of a couple of American dollars. With this money, I was able to buy the tiniest amount of heroin for a momentary high.

Chapter Nine

DESPERATE MEASURES

Here I was, back in my hometown, with nothing. My mother was going frantic with worry, and she spent all her time and money in pursuit of a cure for me. She checked me into hospital many times to no avail. In spite of her devout Catholic faith, she paid for audiences with traditional medicine men. Out of sheer desperation she consulted fortune-tellers and occultists to find a solution to my addiction, and all she got from the people who claim to see into the future and into the past was that an uncle was responsible for my problem, but none of them offered a solution, even though they all claimed they could raise the dead. In fact, she even became a prey to a good number of those she contacted; while each of them proposed a different answer, none of the supposed solutions ever worked. My mother spent money and even sold most of her belongings as these occultists kept on telling her what the gods demanded in order to deliver me from the yoke of drug addiction.

In spite of numerous trips to the hospital, I could not manage to shake my psychological addiction to drugs. I felt that I needed them because I could not live without them. At the same time, I knew that they were stopping me from living, so a strange battle started within my soul. I knew that I needed something more, something else to give meaning to my life, but I didn't know what to do.

I tried anything and everything: I visited witch doctors; I made Juju contracts which promised to free me of my addiction and solve all my problems; I visited herbalists; I went to prayer houses, consulted an imam, and went to all sorts of churches. I was praying for release from my addiction, but perversely I was still praying for the power of divine protection not to allow me to be caught with drugs. Secretly I still wanted to keep dealing drugs. I wanted the money and the prestige, but without being a drug addict. Lots of people I knew made a living from drug dealing without indulging in what they sold. It was possible. My mother thought that I wanted to give up my entire association with the world of drugs, which is why she was spending all her energies helping me, but really I just wanted to be more in control of my smuggling so that I could make more of a profit.

I had been a member of a cult for several years at this point. It began as a part-time affair, whenever I happened to be near one of their branches, but now I started to go to the church very regularly. It dawned on me pretty quickly that it was, in fact, not a real church. It was not Christian. Most of the songs sung during the service were actually in praise of the leader. The congregation was encouraged to believe that the man in charge of this cult was *the* living god, and at the very mention of his name everyone would bow their heads in reverence. This made me very uncomfortable, and I found it difficult to sing the songs as I could not truly believe in the meaning of the words. After one service he kept me back and asked me why I had not been bowing my head during the songs as was expected. I told him that I wasn't comfortable with doing this, and he strongly advised me to watch the other members of the congregation and copy their actions.

One night we were told that there was going to be an appearance of the great leader himself. He would ride into Calabar on a donkey, in the same manner as Christ had entered Jerusalem. We were told to be vigilant and to wait patiently for a glimpse of the leader. When we saw him we would be blessed. So we waited. There was a crowd of us, waiting at the entrance to the church. We waited late into the night. I made sure that I did not close my eyes, so desperately did I want to see the leader and receive his blessing. I did not want to miss this spectacular sight.

I am sure that I did not fall asleep. I kept my eyes wide open, but during the whole night I did not see a thing. As the morning light appeared, people began to disperse, talking excitedly about how the great leader had appeared to them. Adamant that I hadn't seen anything, I asked them when this event was supposed to have occurred. They claimed he had appeared at three o'clock in the morning. I disputed their claim, insisting that it had never happened, that they had imagined it or simply made it up. I knew that I had not seen any such thing. A few days later, the leader got to hear of my dissent, and he had a private word with me. He warned me not to spread false rumors. Just because I had fallen asleep and missed the spectacle, he said, didn't mean that I could deny what other people had seen.

In spite of these obvious discrepancies, the cult professed to offer me protection and the prospect of a way out of the rut I was in. I kept attending in the hope that my material wealth would increase, my luck would return, and that my drug addiction would be cured.

BREAKING TIES

My mother hated the fact that I was a member of this cult. All they did, she said, was encourage people to worship a mortal man, and then take everybody's money in collections for their own use. I tried to persuade her to come to church in Calabar with me and see what it was all about. I told her that people came from as far afield as Europe and the United States just to be at one of these services. They were a very impressive affair, with a huge crowd, and I told her that she would be amazed to see such a sight. She replied that her church was having a prayer meeting at Elele, run by Father Ede. It would not be very big, and the service would be simple, but she would much prefer to go there rather than spend time in a false church with people who did not know God. She asked me to drop her off on my way to Calabar, but when we reached Elele, I was astounded by the sight of a sea of people converging on the place where Father Ede was going to preach. I didn't want to admit it to my mother, but the number of people at Calabar was not even one tenth of the number that came to Elele. The numbers impressed me. I decided to stay for the service out of sheer curiosity.

I managed to push my way to the front. I wanted to see what was happening. There were soldiers forming a security barrier at the front, but somehow I got past them and stood close to Father Ede as he preached. During the service he asked the congregation to raise up any objects that they wanted a blessing for. I watched several people raise their hands. Then he asked for any objects which people wanted destroyed. He said he would "cast them into the archives." People around me were raising things up, and, not wanting to feel like the odd one out, I held up my cult membership card. It caught Father Ede's eye.

"Is this the first time you have been to my prayer ministry?" he asked.

"Yes," I replied.

"Will you please drop the card onto the pulpit," he instructed me. I did, and he sprinkled holy water over my head and onto the card. "That man will come after you," he warned me, speaking about the leader of the cult, "but he cannot kill you."

My mother was elated at the sight of me surrendering my tie to the cult. As soon as we got home she rushed around to tell the entire family of my decision to abandon this false church.

She wanted to make a special journey to Arochukwu in order to tell my grandfather the good news. The next morning she left early, saying that she would return on Easter Monday.

That night my brother Samuel and I were the only ones at the family home. We lived on the third floor of a small housing block. Samuel was in his room, and I lay in my mother's bedroom reading a magazine. Due to the threat of armed robbers, the compound gates were securely locked at 10 P.M. Anyone who was late was simply not allowed in. Much to my surprise, sometime after 11 P.M., I heard what sounded like my mother's voice calling to be let in. Thinking she had missed her bus, I went to the window and looked out, but there was nobody there.

I returned to my magazine. Hearing a soft step in the room, I looked up and was shocked to see the founder of the cult standing before me, dressed in a scarlet cassock. I blinked several times, but the vision did not go away. I was not dreaming. I was wide awake. My skin broke out in goose pimples, and I was terrified. He approached me slowly, but my terror had frozen me. I could not move, and I had no voice to cry out.

"Lawrence, come out from that place," he ordered, speaking of my new conversion to Father Ede's ministry.

"No," I managed to whisper. "I will not."

Furiously he advanced toward where I lay on the bed and pinned me down with such force that I was not able to struggle. I tried to shout for help, but I could not utter a sound, as though my tongue were tied to the roof of my mouth. I even tried to knock the table fan off the dressing table next to the bed so that my brother would come to see what the disturbance was about, but I could not reach it. My legs were numb; I was paralyzed, and I thought that I was going to die.

The man continued to hold me down, his hands tightening around my throat as he slowly choked me. I started mouthing the name, "Jesus" over and over again, until a little sound started to leak from my throat. "Jesus! Jesus!" I whispered, "Jesus!"

His hands dropped from my throat, and I felt movement return to my body. "You cannot kill me!" I shouted, repeating Father Ede's words. "You cannot kill me. I have left you and your cult. You cannot kill me!"

My brother heard my frightened voice and rushed into the room. The man had disappeared. When I told him what had happened he was very scared, knowing of the black magic employed by this kind of people. Nobody ever left this cult and got away with it—the cult did not want to be undermined or have their secrets exposed. They liked their members to be compliant and under control. The founder was a very dangerous man, and we knew that he would not give up. Feeling much shaken, we stayed up all night, unable to sleep, for fear that he might come back. We sat there in the dark, praying for daylight.

The next day I went to see the local priest for guidance. He gave me a rosary to use as a talisman, but advised me to go and see Father Ede who had more experience in dealing with these matters. I said I would go to Elele first thing tomorrow, but it was not soon enough. That very night, the founder returned. I was watching television, wearing the rosary round my neck, and the man appeared in front of me as if from nowhere. Again he tried to strangle me. I felt myself starting to lose consciousness, but in a very tiny voice, I managed to call Jesus' name, and he freed his hold on me. He vanished just as strangely as he had appeared.

It was imperative that I go and seek advice from Father Ede. I did not know how to stop this from happening again. I could only hold onto the comfort he had given me, that this man would not be able to kill me. Nevertheless, he had come pretty close, and I was very scared. Father Ede invited me to come and be a resident of his prayer camp in Elele. There, he said, I would have full protection from the cult leader, and I would be able to concentrate on beating my drug addiction and beginning a new chapter of my life.

My mother was overjoyed that I had gone to stay at the camp. She believed that Father Ede could provide the best advice and teaching for me, and that I was safe in his hands. Indeed, Father Ede strongly urged me to give up all ties to the drug world. He said it was not enough simply to overcome my addiction to drugs, I must also overcome my addiction to the lifestyle of a drug dealer, as no good could come of it. He warned that I would inevitably be arrested if I persisted in peddling drugs, but due to the amazing luck I had experienced so far, I did not heed his words. I continued to believe that I would escape prosecution.

After three months in the camp, I returned home. I was still in the same state, financially, and I found it impossible to continue living on such a small income. Instead of looking for legitimate work, I found it much easier to attempt another drug run. I had a friend who offered to pay me to be a drug mule. I wouldn't have to put up any capital; everything would be arranged in advance. All I had to do was go to India and bring back the drugs. The whole trip would take just over a week. Little did I know that it would be over seventeen years before I would return home.

Chapter Ten

ONE LAST TRIP

My friend had planned everything. This was around 1990. He had recruited a sex worker to pose as my partner, who would travel to India with me and help to carry some of the consignment. Fake passports had been hurriedly made for both of us: each passport had a different name and fake information to prevent us from being identified. One passport was to take us to India, and the other passport—stamped with my fake Italian immigration stamp—was to be presented in Lagos on the way back to cover our tracks. If the Nigerian customs officials saw that we had travelled to India for such a brief period, they would be more likely to check our bags and have us searched. We needed to be as careful as possible not to draw attention to ourselves. After all, we would only get paid if the drugs were delivered safely, and I really needed the money. Everything was riding on the success of this trip.

The girl was coached on what to say when we reached Rome, in the event that officials wanted to ask her any questions. She also had to pretend to know me very well and act like my long-term girlfriend, even though we had only just met. I would do most of the talking for both of us, but she had to know what to say just in case we were separated and interviewed individually. Our stories would have to match up.

Going to India was fine. Everything went according to plan. We left on a Monday from Nigeria, and spent three days in India, checking the consignment, carefully ingesting it, and then preparing to fly. We each swallowed one kilo of heroin, wrapped in ovules of ten grams each, as was standard. Our flight from Bombay was on time, and we landed in Rome early on Thursday morning. When we reached immigration, I handed in my passport and waited while they checked the dates of my visit to India. As expected, they asked me why I had spent such a short time in the country, and I told them my prepared answer. It seemed so plausible that they let me through without any further questions, and I went to the transfer lounge to wait for my partner.

The minutes ticked by, and I glanced at my watch—I had been waiting for nearly half an hour. I got up and took a stroll, picking up one of the free newspapers on offer. I needed something to occupy me during this tense wait. What was going on? When I had been reading and rereading the same page of my newspaper for about an hour, I began to grow very uncomfortable. There was no way it should have taken her this long. Suddenly, over the announcement system, I heard my name being called out. I was to come to the information desk at once where airport police would be waiting for me.

The worst had happened, I thought. The game was up. There was nowhere to run to. I couldn't exit the airport without going through immigration. I did not have my other passport on me. The girl had them both. Immigration would certainly prevent me from boarding the flight to Lagos, and there was no way I could get the drugs out of my system before my unavoidable interview with the airport police. The only thing to do was to pretend that I didn't know what they were talking about. Maybe I could bluff my way through this crisis.

It turned out that the other passport had generated the suspicion that had fallen upon me. The girl, faced with the scrutiny of the Italian immigration officers, had fluffed her lines. She had not been able to remember her story under pressure; she had hesitated, and her answers were inconsistent. Immediately, the officers had searched her clothes and luggage. Finding nothing incriminating there, they had called the police who had taken her to the local hospital for an x-ray. They found all the drugs they were expecting to find inside her stomach. What they weren't expecting to find were two fake passports tucked inside her underwear. And one of those passports had my photo on it.

I was taken to the hospital as well and was rushed into the x-ray department. Knowing that they would find the drugs eventually, I resigned myself to discovery. The x-rays were studied, but, amazingly, the drugs did not show up. Puzzled, the officers tried to work out why I would be travelling with a girl who had a kilo of heroin inside her and smuggled fake passports in her underwear, but did not carry any of the drugs myself. Was I her pimp? Was I related to her? Was I supposed to pick up some more drugs in Italy? Was I meeting anybody at the airport? They questioned me repeatedly, trying to get an explanation. They asked me about the passports, and reminded me that possession of a fake document carried a prison sentence of its own. I would be arrested anyway, even if they did not find the drugs, but now their curiosity was aroused, and they wanted to know the full story.

One of the officers suggested that I be x-rayed again. According to him, it was impossible that I was not carrying any drugs. It would be stupid to carry two passports just for the sake of it.

There had to be a reason behind my deception—and drugs seemed to be the obvious connection. The second x-ray yielded different results. The ovules had travelled further along my digestive tract and now appeared much more obvious in the pictures. They could clearly see the packets in my stomach. There was no further deliberation. I had been caught red-handed for the first time in my life. I remembered Rev. Father Ede's warning that I would be caught, prosecuted, and jailed if I continued dealing drugs. My luck had finally run out.

We were escorted by police to a private room in the hospital, and there we were handcuffed to the metal frames of our beds. Guards were stationed outside the door to the room, and a guard sat by our side. Every time we needed to pass an ovule, the guard would hand us a little metal container. From there, the ovules were put into plastic bags as evidence. We were not allowed to leave the room at all, every movement being scrutinized by the guards. It seemed like an eternity; in all probability, it went on for several days. The days started to blur into each other, and I lost track of time. The guards had been instructed to wait until all the ovules had been passed, and then we were to be brought to the prison where we would stay until the date of our trial. When they thought they had the entire stash, we were bundled off into police cars. That was the last I ever saw of the girl.

I spent some time in prison before I was called to sentencing. In my possession were two ovules of heroin that had somehow escaped the notice of the police. This small amount of drugs got me through that initial tough time and made me a few friends in the cells. I did not want to think about what would happen after that twenty grams ran out. I did not want to think ahead at all. I was in a strange country; I knew no one; and now that I was in prison I had no way of getting out. I had always been used to having a life on the move. I had been free to go where I wanted, do what I wanted, to travel extensively and keep active. Now I was confined within four walls, day after day after endless day. My life had come to a standstill, and I wondered if I could sink any lower.

On my way to sentencing I was transferred from the cells in a van with another prisoner, an Italian guy, charged with theft. He was amazed that I had been working as a drug trafficker for so long because, in his opinion, it was one of the most dangerous and risky of all criminal enterprises. He offered to induct me into the ways of professional robbery in order to give me an alternative to the drug world, but I vehemently refused. I was appalled that he could consider his profession superior to mine. In my country, stealing was seen as the lowest of all vices and would not be tolerated. Even though I was a felon, convicted of drug smuggling and possession of heroin, I still judged this man to be more disgraceful than me! It is amazing that I could be so hypocritical, but at that time I still saw drug smuggling as just another way of making money. In spite of my arrest and the humiliation I had suffered at the hands of the Italian police, I still could not admit how terrible my drug-fuelled existence was.

PRISONER IN A STRANGE LAND

I was sentenced to four years. Overnight my life changed into one of captivity. Like an animal, I lived only for the satisfaction of my most primitive needs. I was jolted awake by the loud ringing of alarms and listened to the sound of prisoners banging on the bars of their cells. It was breakfast time. The smell of cheap, watery porridge drifted along the corridors, and it was delivered to the cells with the accompaniment of stale bread. Mingled with these comparatively luxurious odors, was the stench of urine and excrement. I felt sick and suddenly very cold. My body was cramped and sore. I had been curled up on a bed too small for a grown man to sleep on. The brick walls were chipped, scratched, and scored in dozens of places, and the paint was peeling off. There was not much light.

The footsteps of guards echoed in the corridors as they marched past my cell. It was a sobering thought that they held the keys to my release. From now on, my life would be dictated by them. The nights were always the hardest. Being locked into a small space by yourself without anyone to talk to was almost unbearable. I quickly found a way to get hold of drugs. Without drugs I would not have been able to cope. They made everything easier. When I was high I did not have to face up to the reality which surrounded me. I could escape from the nightmare of the prison in a euphoric dream. Having access to drugs also meant having friends. Even though they were the most superficial of friendships, it was nice to create the illusion that you were not alone and that people cared about you.

During the day, once I had been let out into the main prison complex, things were not so bad. I kept myself as busy as possible to stave off the boredom, taking up any work that was available to prisoners. There were quite a few schemes implemented by the prison authorities, including a small clothes-making business, which enabled me to make a little bit of money. This I gave to the wife of a fellow prisoner, who came to visit her husband every week, and promised to wire it to my mother in Nigeria. It was only later that I discovered that the money had never reached its destination, but at the time I really believed that I was doing something to help my family and make up for the years of neglect.

Amazingly enough, my luck hadn't quite run out. I made it through the first six months without too much trouble and found at the end of it that somebody had made a mistake in the appeal process, which resulted in my premature release. I was ejected from the prison rather unceremoniously, and left to do what I liked on the streets of Rome. The only problem was that I had nothing. I had no passport, no identity documents of any kind. I had only the clothes that I had worn in prison. I had nowhere to go; I knew nobody in the city; and I had no money.

It was winter, and the weather was particularly cold. I wandered around looking for shelter, and as it grew dark and the temperature dropped even further, I became desperate. In the end, I shut myself into a phone booth and hunched down on the floor, trying to get warm. I managed to sleep like that for a few hours, and stayed there until morning. There were only two options for the day ahead, I thought. If I wanted to eat and find somewhere to sleep, then I had to either steal or beg. So I begged.

It was clear that Rome was far too expensive to be hospitable to a penniless Nigerian, and there was no way I could afford to buy a plane ticket back home, even if I did manage to get a new passport—which, nevertheless, I could not afford either. I heard that Padova (Padua) was the place to be if you were Nigerian. There were quite a few Nigerians and other Africans there, and they banded together in order to survive. There were opportunities for work there, it was said, and when I had scraped together enough for a cheap bus ticket, to Padova I went.

The rumors of work were exaggerated, but the number of Nigerians was not. There were plenty of my countrymen, and from then on I was never on my own again. The only problem was finding enough work for all of us. We would scavenge for things to sell, or get cheap things off the black market—novelty cigarette lighters, cheap underwear, key rings, and suchlike. Things people didn't really need. We would converge on the piazza at dawn to join the Italian women selling food at market stalls, and we would all try to sell things to people who didn't want them. It was challenging enough as it was, but as the numbers of poor and homeless people grew, the less room there was for another hawker. The market became saturated with *venditore ambulante* (mobile sellers). We moved from place to place whenever the sales dried up, not that there were many sales.

Between us we made enough money to buy food and small amounts of drugs, but not enough money to pay for accommodation. We slept on the street, but in the cold winter weather we took to sleeping on buses, snatching a few hours whenever we could, sitting upright in our seats. It was such a common sight to see numerous black people asleep on public transport, gently nodding to the rhythm of the engine. It was warmer on the buses, packed in with all those other people. Much better than freezing to death outside.

With me, though, it was the same old story. I just couldn't make enough money to pay for the amount of drugs that I really wanted. In my head I *needed* more drugs. In my mind I could not live without them. So the only way to make a bigger profit was to return to drug dealing. Through the Nigerians who had been in Padova for a while, I was able to make some connections and get started. My business was nothing on the scale of what I had previously done. It was just small-time drug peddling to make a little cash. The cash was immediately spent on drugs, and then the whole cycle would start again. Now that I had friends, I had somewhere to stay, so homelessness was no longer an issue. I could concentrate all my energies on making enough money to satisfy my drug habit.

If I had wanted to, I suppose I could have scrimped and saved the money to return home, but from then on my sole occupation was keeping myself supplied with drugs. There was no room for any other thought. The return to Nigeria could wait.

POLIZIA OR PULIZIA?

I was in and out of prison plenty of times for small drug offences. Over the coming years I would lose track of the number of times I was arrested and sentenced. Sometimes the time I served would be short—only a few weeks or months—but other times I would be back in for years. I was so frequently questioned by police that I actively avoided them. If they were patrolling the area, I would hide until the coast was clear. The police haunted me in my dreams. Sometimes, walking down the street, I would imagine that I saw a police officer out of the corner of my eye, following me, watching me.

My paranoia was so great that one day, holding a stash of drugs for a customer in a cheap hotel, I started to think there were police waiting outside the door. My client was due to pick up the drugs in a couple of hours, and until his arrival, all I could do was pace nervously up and down the room. Before the appointed time, a knock came at the door. It was too early to be my client, but I did not want to open the door to check. I remained silent, hoping that the person would go away.

"Pulizia! Pulizia!" cried a voice at the door, and the person knocked again. *"Pulizia!"*

I trembled, thinking immediately of the consequences of a police search. I did not want to go back into prison. Rushing to the bathroom, I hurriedly tipped the whole stash down the toilet and flushed the chain. With the evidence disposed of, I ran back into the room and pretended I had just woken up. Faking a yawn, I opened the door. To my horror, the person that stood there was an elderly woman in a maid's uniform. Instead of the terrifying *polizia* (police) I had been afraid of nothing but a harmless *pulizia* (cleaner).

I screamed at her, calling her all sorts of horrendous names, and the poor woman just stared at me as if I were mad. Of course she had no idea how much her interruption had cost me, and I could not explain. I had lost a valuable stash and a good customer. And I had made nothing.

MERRY-GO-ROUND

Here I was again, just being released from another stretch in prison. The years had begun to blend into each other, the sentences were all the same—different lengths and different prisons, but essentially the same. I bought drugs; I sold drugs; I was arrested for selling drugs. The same events repeated themselves again and again. Up to now, I had always expected to be released and to pick up where I had left off, slotting back easily into my routine of dealing and drug using. But on one occasion in 1999, things did not go as I expected.

Olusegun Obasanjo, then President of Nigeria, had made a visit to Italy earlier that year, and requested that the Italian government deport any Nigerian who had been convicted of drug-related offences or prostitution. On my release from prison, instead of being left on the street as usual, I was transported to a detention camp in Torino (Turin). There I was made particularly conspicuous by being the only person transferred directly from prison. All the others had been out for some time. There were many other Nigerians in the camp, all desperate to avoid deportation. For some, being in Italy was the only way to make a decent amount of money to feed their poor family back home. For others, it was the only life they knew—back in Nigeria they had nothing.

My roommate was a fellow Nigerian, and he tried to comfort me. He had been there before, in that very camp, and had been released after thirty days. They wouldn't deport us, he said. But I wasn't so sure. He had never been to prison. He was only there because his papers were not in order. I, on the other hand, had a terrible record of drug offences. I had been in prison so many times that it had become a second home to me. Why would the Italian immigration officials even consider letting me stay in their country? I dreaded going home to face my family, especially in this disgraceful way. I was too ashamed even to think about it. Every day I caused my mother grief. My grandmother had died in my absence, thinking the worst of me. I had lied to everyone, cheated them, and let them down. There was nothing I could do to redeem myself. I had sunk as low as it was possible to go.

Every morning we would hear the wailing and screaming of people who were about to be deported. Wherever they were from in the world, whatever language they spoke, the sound was always the same: despair. It was a terrible environment to be in. There was no sense of hope. My roommate tried his best to be optimistic, but I found it impossible. Some people went to great lengths to avoid deportation, to the extent of risking their own lives. One girl pretended to be mad, tore her clothes, and ran naked and screaming around the camp. The authorities did not bat an eyelid. They had seen it all before. Instead of calming her down and letting her stay as she thought they would, they caught her, injected her with sedatives, and she woke up hours later at Lagos International Airport. There were other people who slit their wrists, or cut themselves in other places, hoping that their injuries would prevent them from being deported. The authorities would have none of it. I did not believe that I stood a chance. I had visions of turning up destitute in Lagos, being taken from the airport to prison, and having to beg from my family for bail money. The thought was too embarrassing to bear.

It turned out that this time my roommate was sent back to Nigeria. He called ahead to let his sister know so that she could help him out when he arrived, and he wished me luck. I sat and waited. Day after day I sat worrying about what would happen to me, and it was then that I remembered God. As a last resort, I prayed not to be sent back. I prayed for my release. I prayed long and hard, without really thinking. I prayed out of fear and desperation. But there was an answer. Quite unexpectedly, I was released from the detention camp after thirty days, which was the maximum length of time they could hold anybody there without further action being taken against them. I was amazed. The officials at the camp were dumbfounded. The Camp Inspector said that in all his time of working at the camp, he had never seen anything like it. He thought it was a miracle, as I was such an unlikely candidate for release.

I was now in Turin. It was a different city, very different from Padua or Rome, but I acted the same. As soon as I was released from the camp, I found out where I could buy cocaine and heroin. I sat in a stranger's apartment that evening, smoking. I got high and left the apartment to go for a walk. Minutes later a fight broke out between a couple of addicts, and the police were called. If I hadn't left when I did, I would have ended up back in the detention camp that same evening. I had a very lucky escape. It should have hit me then, the mindless way I kept going back to drugs and repeating the same mistakes over and over again, but it didn't. I just didn't think about it. It should have made me want to turn over a new leaf and begin again, but all I thought about was my next fix. It seemed I was a hopeless junkie, doomed to ride an endless merry-go-round.

Chapter Eleven

AT THE END OF MYSELF

Prison became my home—not even my second home, but my first. I didn't have anywhere else. I would be let out one morning, only to end up back in my cell the same evening. My face was familiar to all the prison guards, and they used to joke about when they would see me again. Usually they wouldn't have to wait long. The inevitable return to the small concrete cell, with the same scratches and scrawling on the walls and the same stale, dank air, began to get to me. I became very depressed. Even though I knew drugs were responsible for my times in prison, I still couldn't resist the temptation. The more despondent I became, the more I hated my life and my addiction, the more I needed that intense and momentary high that heroin would give me.

It's been said that "insanity is doing the same thing, over and over again, and expecting different results." I don't know if I thought drugs would help me, but I kept turning to them as a solution. Of course, they only made me increasingly unhappy and paranoid the more I took them. Every time I came down from a high, the low would hit me so hard that I wanted to kill myself. I started to lose my grip on reality, and paranoia had such a stranglehold on me that I hovered on the brink of insanity.

I had long felt that there was something missing—that my life lacked meaning and purpose—but throughout all my travels and adventures I had found nothing to fill the darkness of that void. I began to question the point of living at all. Any relationships I had were empty and one-sided. I wasn't interested in being intimate with anyone, but I wouldn't allow the woman to see anybody else, so of course, these women would not put up with me for very long. All I wanted to do was sit around and smoke cocaine and heroin.

Carmella was a feisty Italian lady with a very strong character. She ran a bar in downtown Rovigo, near Padua, but also sold drugs to wealthy businessmen and politicians, making plenty of money. Our relationship was a clash of egos—both of us were looking to control each other. We each used a lot of cocaine and worked together to sell it. I supplied her with the coke, and she would use her influence to market it to her best clients. We would spend all night getting high and gained the reputation of being a reckless, drugged-up couple. It was a recipe for disaster, as we were both very jealous people. One night my paranoia took me over the edge.

We were both attending a party that I had been paid to emcee. I spotted the girlfriend of a friend I used to know and went over to chat to her. Carmella watched me laughing and talking with the lady and stormed over, shouting, "Oh, so you want to show me that you have another girl, huh?"

Before I could explain who the lady was, she had gone right up to another man and started dancing with him. She looked at me, as if to say, "Two can play at that game." Not being able to control my temper, I immediately flew into a rage and pushed my way over to where she was dancing. I shoved the other man out of the way and grabbed Carmella by the hair. She screamed in pain, but I did not release her. Instead I dragged her right out of the bar and into the street. She slapped me in the face to make me let go of her, but this just made me even more angry. I completely lost control of myself and started hitting her as hard as I could. I tore her dress off so I could land blows on her bare skin. She was crying out that I had drawn blood, but I did not stop. It was as though I was possessed. I had no self-control or compassion. I just wanted to make her hurt.

I was stopped by several police officers who had been called to the scene. They had caught me red-handed and put me straight into the car to be taken to the station. An ambulance was called, and the last I saw of Carmella was her battered body lying on the ground. She was covered in blood, and my hands were red with the stuff. I heard later that she needed nearly two months of treatment in hospital before she was finally able to go home. I felt disgusted with myself. I was irrational, selfish, and a danger to others. It suddenly occurred to me that I did not deserve to live anymore.

In prison once more, I could not sleep. I felt as though I were going mad. The prison medics prescribed sleeping pills, but instead of taking them, I stored them up for future use. Morning and evening the nurses would come round with these little pills, and both times I just pretended to take them. After several weeks I had almost a full bottle, and before going to bed one night I took the whole lot. They were strong and took effect instantly. I fell down on the floor of the cell with the cigarette I had been smoking still smoldering in my hand. The cigarette rolled out of my fingers and toward my tracksuit where it proceeded to set fire to my clothing. Oblivious to the smoke and the burning, I lay there on the concrete floor waiting for death.

The smoke was spotted by a couple of wardens who were distributing the meals that evening. They raised the alarm and guards quickly came to my cell to carry me to the hospital where I was kept on suicide watch for the following twenty-four hours. After that I was given another sentence for attempted suicide while on my previous sentence. It seemed that I was destined to live out my days in prison.

From Padua I was transferred to Rovigo, then on to Pordenone, and finally ended up in Belluno. There a ray of hope shone upon me in the form of a woman. It was early in 1995. One of my teachers at the prison introduced me to a lady called Angela who became a good friend to me during my sentence. She would visit me regularly and waited patiently for my release so that we could have a normal relationship. Angela was a traditional Roman Catholic, and her mother was firmly against this undesirable relationship for her only daughter—not only because I was an ex-convict, but also because I was black. There was a lot of racism in Italy at the time, but Angela didn't care about anything except the fact that she loved me. She could look beyond the drug addiction and the prison sentence. She really wanted to help me lead a normal life, and she sought to heal my broken soul with her affection and her faith. I liked her very much and started to imagine how different my life would be with a good woman by my side. Dismissing the concerns of her family and friends, Angela accepted my proposal, and we were married just over a month after I was released from prison.

For a few months everything was wonderful, and the future began to look very bright. We made lots of plans to settle down together and start a family, make a new life for ourselves, but before long, my drug addiction began to be a problem. She was firmly against using drugs and was very clean-living. If I had followed her example then, perhaps I would have been happier, but her refusal to indulge my drug habit meant that I felt suffocated, banned from enjoying the only thing I really loved in life. I had to sneak out to do drugs as she would not allow me to have them in the house, and I had to constantly hide my addiction from her to keep our marriage harmonious. Now that I can look back with a clear head, I realize that she truly loved me, and that she did everything to try to help me, but she did not have the power to save me. She thought that once she married me I would make a clean break, but in fact I was effectively married to drugs. It broke her heart.

On our three-month wedding anniversary we were meant to be celebrating but ended up having a small argument; I don't remember what about. It was so minor, but my temper flared once again, and I beat her. I immediately regretted it, but nothing I could say would make it up to her. It was too late for apologies. She had seen the man I really was, and she did not like what she saw.

I went crazy and began taking all the drugs I could find. I emptied the medicine cabinet, the first aid box, searched all the cupboards and swallowed whole bottles of pills and all the painkillers in sight. There must have been nearly a hundred tablets in all—I just kept putting them in my mouth until I couldn't swallow any more. Angela had run out of the room, so I shouted to her that I was going to kill her and then myself. Taking a large kitchen knife, I went after her, but she managed to flee from the house before I could find her and harm her. The pills were slowing me down now, and I felt groggy. I had no idea what I had taken, but I just wanted to end it all. Now that Angela had gone, there was nothing to live for. I took the knife and plunged it into my stomach, hoping to bleed to death. I fell to the floor and passed out.

This is how the police found me. Angela had called them as soon as she had reached safety, and they came to the house to make sure I would not hurt anybody else. I woke up in hospital in Belluno. The knife wound had been stitched up, but I would be forever left with an ugly, jagged scar to remind me of how I had almost become a murderer. I was kept in hospital for a few days before being transferred to the all-too-familiar Belluno courtroom. There I was informed of a restraining order placed upon me that would prevent me from ever going near Angela, thereby protecting both her and her family. I was anguished to think of the pain I had caused her, and to think that my newly wedded wife never wanted to see me again.

WANTING TO DIE

A voice kept telling me to do it. As soon as I was out of hospital I heard it, whispering to me, suggesting that the only way out was to kill myself. It would not leave me alone. I tried to ignore it, but every time I was driving a car, the urge would come over me to veer off the road. I was surrounded by a permanent darkness wherever I went. My soul was in shadow. Italians call it *"il male oscuro"*—"the invisible sickness." For me, that perfectly describes the alienation of depression. People would look at me and think I was fine, but inside I was dying.

I desperately wanted to put an end to my life, but in the back of my mind was the stigma carried by suicide in my country. It would mean that my body would not be repatriated; I would not be able to be buried in Nigeria, and the whole thing would bring unimaginable shame and grief to my family. But if I could manage to set up my suicide to look like an accident…it would be better for everyone. A car crash was the most obvious choice; it could happen so easily, and nobody could prove that I had done it deliberately. I began to be obsessed with the idea. The devilish voice in my head focused on this and egged me on.

The wound on my stomach was still fresh, the stitches having been put in less than a week ago. I had embarked on a smoking spree that lasted all night, and then, while still high, I got in the car to drive home to the apartment where I now lived alone. It was about two o'clock in the morning, and the roads were almost deserted. Suddenly I heard a very clear voice saying, "Do it now! Do it now!" Immediately, and without question, I obeyed, veering off the road into the bushes. I was going quite fast, and the car shot through the bushes into a ditch on the other side.

I was knocked out. The whole front of the car was smashed in, and the vehicle was a complete write-off. Being unconscious, I was not aware of the fact that I had plunged head first into a ditch full of water. Very quickly, the car filled up with me inside it. If it hadn't been for the quick thinking of the driver behind me on the road who had witnessed the "accident," I would have drowned. He called the police and the ambulance services who pulled me to safety and revived me. I was taken to Treviso hospital with minor injuries. It is amazing that I did not sustain anything worse considering the speed I had been going at. I did not want to talk to the doctors about my experience, so I refused to be admitted and discharged myself from hospital. They asked me to sign a form consenting to treatment if anything more serious were to happen. Obviously they had their suspicions about my mental state, but instead of letting them help me I just turned back to drugs to take away the pain.

Over the next couple of years the voice in my head kept urging me to take my life, usually while driving. I had so many road accidents that I destroyed five cars in less than four years. In spite of my high accident rate, nobody thought to question me about how they had happened. I suppose my reputation for drug abuse and general recklessness explained it sufficiently to the authorities, but in truth I don't think anybody really cared. If I had died, I don't think any of my so-called friends would have missed me. Between prison, smoking and drug peddling I did not have much time for friends anyway. My life was an empty cycle of punishment and self-harm. Yet sometimes it is only in darkness that you can see the light.

Chapter Twelve

SALVATION

Help came from the most unexpected quarter. It came from prison! Things were looking very bleak. After only three months on the outside, I was thrown back into jail in 2001 for supply and possession of cocaine. I had lost my head in court and answered back to the judge, lecturing him on the pointlessness of going after small-time drug dealers when the big drug barons and mafia types carried on scot-free. He was furious with me, in spite of the fact that what I said was essentially true. I was in contempt of court, he said, and as a result, I deserved to be transferred to Caltanissetta, a notorious punishment jail, where I would be more likely to learn my lesson.

Caltanissetta was horrible. There was constant surveillance and perpetual humiliation. Each time you wanted to leave your cell for some fresh air, or visit the toilet or the infirmary, you would be forced to undress and display your front and backside to the guards, just to prove that you were not hiding any weapons. In addition, you would be accompanied everywhere by two guards, one on each side. I tried to stay in my cell as much as possible so that I would not give the guards the satisfaction of strip-searching me. Rather than endure this kind of ritual humiliation for any length of time, I planned to kill myself.

These thoughts of suicide were fortunately diverted by a new friend I made in prison. His name was Michael, and he was serving a very long sentence for the possession of a small amount of cocaine. By the time I arrived, he had been in Caltanissetta for nearly ten years. It didn't seem fair, considering the amount of drugs I frequently carried and used. I had never been in prison for more than two years at a stretch in spite of everything I had done, whereas this had been Michael's first offence. He was a friendly person, very easy to get on with, and he immediately started giving me good advice. He had noticed the way I chain-smoked to keep calm and was concerned that I was a slave to cigarettes. I had gradually cut down on using heroin and cocaine during this most recent sentence because in Caltanissetta it wasn't possible to smuggle hard drugs inside. The guards were much too vigilant. Instead, I relied heavily on cigarettes and, when really desperate, I sniffed glue, or the fumes from the small gas stoves we used to cook on.

"Solution," he said to me one day, "You smoke too much."

"I know that already," I replied. I also knew that it was almost impossible for me to give it up, even for a day, and I told him so.

"You obviously haven't requested the visit of the best physician," he said.

I was indignant, telling him that I had tried all sorts of rehab centers and hospitals. I had seen all the best doctors in Italy and had even gone out with a lady doctor once who had made sure that I was admitted to a renowned hospital for treatment. None of them had managed to help me. In fact, after the last failed attempt to come clean in a rehab center, my addiction had become even worse than it was before. I had lost all hope of a cure.

"I meant Doctor Jesus," he smiled, pointing up to the ceiling.

"Do you think you know God better than me?" I asked him furiously. "I knew God before you ever did."

"Solution," he calmly said to me, "I believe you knew God before me. I only came to know God inside prison, but I can assure you that God is real and His Son Jesus is alive." He then asked if I would agree to let him pray with me. He was confident that Jesus would give me the strength to conquer my addiction to smoking.

I laughed, as I had just lit a fresh cigarette, but I laid it down on the table so that I could give him both my hands to pray over. I decided that it wouldn't hurt, and Michael seemed so passionate and convinced that I didn't want to hurt his feelings by refusing. I sat there hoping that it wouldn't be a long prayer so that I could finish smoking my cigarette. It felt odd not having one between my fingers.

As Michael held my hand, he spoke a simple prayer. He asked in Jesus' name for God to set me free from my addiction. And he asked that I be set free *today*. I was just happy that the whole thing didn't take very long, and as soon as he had finished praying, I reached out my hand for the cigarette which was still burning. I picked it up and brought it to my mouth, but as soon as it touched my lips, it fell to the floor. Rather than pick it up again I chose instead to crush it with my shoe. The extinguished stub lay there in front of me, a testament to this new and unfamiliar decision. God had given me the strength to finally say no to cigarettes.

"Michael," I said, looking down at the dirty cigarette butt, "I just got the feeling that I will not smoke again." I didn't understand this feeling, but I knew that it was right.

"That is the Holy Spirit," Michael replied, as casually as if he had been talking about a fly on the wall. To him it was not a surprise, as he had complete faith. He must have known that God would answer his prayer.

From that day, March 21, 2001, I decided that with God's help I would no longer be an addict. I took the responsibility of making the right decisions and following the good path. It became apparent that I could use my experience to help others who were suffering from the same bondage to drugs, and I told God that I was willing to go wherever He might send me so that I could share my testimony with them. Overnight I was transformed from a despondent and reckless drug addict to a hopeful and fulfilled addict of the Word of God.

Michael handed me a copy of *Believer's Voice of Victory* magazine, from Kenneth Copeland Ministries (KCM). It was the first time I had ever heard of Kenneth Copeland. I had never read a Christian publication before, considering them to be pointless. I thought that anyone who proclaimed himself to have been "born again" had simply been brainwashed and was not thinking clearly. Now, as I read all the joyful testimonies in the magazine, I came to realize the power of God's love to change lives and help people start living in freedom and happiness. I realized that I was a valued person; I realized that God loved me; I realized that I had a bright future if I would only follow God and live right. It suddenly seemed so simple. After a short encounter with a true believer, I was filled with the Holy Spirit and full of hope.

I shared a cell with three other prisoners, one Italian and two Tunisians. Up to this point we had all smoked together, and I had freely given them my cigarettes of which I had a large supply. This particular day was different. I went back to my cell and asked the Italian to empty my locker of all the cigarettes he found in there as I was not going to be using them again. He looked at me incredulously, not believing that I was serious. Sometimes people would make these empty statements to demonstrate a willpower that they didn't really have, and he must have thought that my new resolution would be short-lived because he didn't bother to empty the locker.

When I came back from an hour of exercise in the prison yard, I emptied the locker myself. I distributed all the cigarettes amongst my fellow prisoners, telling them to help themselves. In the back of my mind I heard that voice again, the voice I used to hear telling me to harm myself. This time it was saying that I was throwing money away, that those people were now smoking my money, and that I should stop them before it was all gone. I ignored the voice and continued giving away the packets of cigarettes.

Then the devilish voice tried another tack. "You have already smoked today," it said. "So why don't you start afresh tomorrow?" The voice kept nagging me to have another cigarette, contending that I wasn't really clean because I had been smoking just that morning. But God had shown me that with His help I could resist this temptation if I wanted to.

To everyone else I was still a junkie. My cellmates were skeptical, not believing that I would be able to say no to heroin if I was offered it. They fully expected me to return to a life of drugs as soon as I got out of prison. In fact, they probably expected me to die of an overdose one day. The only friends I had were the type of people who were only happy to see you if you brought drugs along. If you were down-and-out, they would shut the door in your face. Nobody I had met during the course of my drug-centered life so far would believe in me.

I had been lucky to have had very restricted access to hard drugs during my recent spell in prison so that I did not get the chance to use them very often. It certainly spared me the agonies of going "cold turkey." Now that I knew I could turn my back on smoking cigarettes, I knew that I could do the same for other drugs. As the days went on, I was amazed to find that my cravings subsided, and that my mental and physical dependence on drugs faded. As the days turned into weeks, my cellmates were forced to admit that I was a changed man. They said it was a miracle that Solution, the "human chimney," was no longer puffing out smoke. I was free!

LIVING THE WORD

With the removal of my addiction, there suddenly appeared room in my life for other things. I actually had the capacity to think of something other than drugs and where to get the money for my next fix. From living on the street and selling everything I owned to feed my craving for drugs, I had moved on to a place of spiritual richness which allowed me to have better and more meaningful priorities. I became totally hooked on the Bible, which provided hours of encouragement and advice. Sometimes I had to be called for meals because I was so absorbed in my reading! Before long I had read the whole thing from cover to cover.

My fellow inmates started to avoid me, as I could not help trying to get them to change their ways and desist from their lives of crime. They could not stand to hear me preaching. I did not mean to drive them away, but I wanted to share my experience with everyone I met, and I wanted them to be filled with the same sense of hope as I now had. In spite of being shunned by the other prisoners, I did not feel lonely. I was able to find a wonderful correspondent in Andrew Prescott, the coordinator of the European branch of the KCM Prison Ministry. He wrote to me regularly, and that meant I had a true friend on the outside. His letters were full of the talk of miracles, which at first I found pretty hard to believe in. I thought the days of miracles were over, but it was not long before I came to see my own deliverance from criminality and addiction as a miracle. Whatever anybody might say (and I know there are many out there who are skeptical about God or even hostile to the idea of salvation), I knew that I could not have done this without Jesus. He opened my eyes to the possibilities of a better life and gave me the strength to make the change. God turned the mess of my life into a message for others, and I sincerely wanted to help other addicts and prisoners by telling them my story.

Not long after Michael had shared his own message with me, he was released from prison. It was an unexpected happy event. I was moved into his former cell, which was smaller than the one I had been used to, with only two occupants. This gave me more privacy to read and study as I wished without interruption. I had many problems to work through. What had previously bothered me to distraction and triggered the most painful migraines, I gradually began to entrust to God. I was still learning how to pray properly and how to rely on the Lord, and sometimes I could not see a way out even with this assistance. I did not know what was going to happen to me after I came out of prison. All I could do was trust that God would provide opportunities for me to move forward with my life on the outside. I had an expulsion order hanging over my head, which meant that I would be deported to Nigeria immediately upon release. This was not very desirable for me as I had not had any chance to rebuild my life and I wanted to make some changes before I saw my family again. I certainly didn't want to be thrown into prison by the Nigerian government after I had just finished a jail sentence in Italy.

I switched out the light one night and got into the top bunk. My Senegalese cellmate was asleep in the bottom bunk. Just as I was drifting off to sleep, I heard a voice say "Romans Ten, Eleven." Startled, I looked around me, but obviously there was nobody else in the room. I thought I must have imagined it, so I tried to get to sleep again. Once more I heard the voice, quite loudly this time, saying, "Romans Ten, Eleven." It was then that I jumped up and switched on the light, which woke up my cellmate. He asked me angrily why I was disturbing his sleep, and I apologized, telling him that I would not be long but that there was something that I absolutely had to do.

Not yet familiar with the order of books in the Bible, I had to search the index page for Romans, but quickly found it. Turning to chapter ten, verse eleven in the King James Bible, I read, "Whosoever believeth on him shall not be ashamed."

My faith rose on reading those words, and I knew that I should not worry about what would happen after I was released from prison. Whatever happened, I would not be ashamed, and I knew that someday I would be able to return to my family with my head held high—all because of God. Little did I know that the route I would take to be reunited with them would be a long and winding one.

First came the order that I was to be transferred out of Caltanissetta. As much as I hated the place, I was angry to be moved with only a few months left of my sentence. I thought that the guards were persecuting me. I was put on a bus to another jail where I was in transit for two days. Then on to another jail for a few days, and yet another, before finally I was made an inmate of a prison in Sardinia. I was very tired, and I was told that I would spend another two weeks behind bars before I was released. This move seemed very pointless to me, especially if they were just going to deport me anyway, but my anger did nothing to help my situation. I just had to trust God that I would not be taken back to Nigeria before I was ready.

Two weeks later I was taken to the local police station where a car had been prepared to take me to the airport. I took my Bible along with me, reading it in the police car. One of the policemen commented that I would be in Lagos in eight hours time. On arrival at the police station, a guard was brought to supervise me until the convoy left for the airport. He said exactly the same thing as the other policeman had said:

"You'll be in Lagos in another eight hours."

"That's what they said," I replied, still reading my Bible.

"So you already know, and you are so calm?" He was amazed. He had been expecting me to put up a fight, to try to escape. He pointed to a broken pane of glass in the office window which, he told me, had been smashed by another Nigerian man who was desperate to avoid deportation. I asked him if this act of vandalism had prevented the man from being deported, and he shook his head.

I pointed to a couple of select verses in my Italian Bible, including the line in the Book of Peter which says, "Cast your cares upon the Lord, for He cares for you." He asked me whether the Word of God really works, to which I replied that I believed so. Even in the face of deportation I still believed that God would use my life for the good. If I had to go to prison in Lagos, then it was because I could help somebody there, just as I was trying to help somebody now. It would not be wasted time. As soon as I had realized that God gives only good things, and can use even the worst situations for His good, I felt so much calmer and could face the future without worry or anger.

The guard and I got to talking, and he confessed several personal problems that were troubling him. He allowed me to pray for him and then said that he felt much better, thanking me for taking an interest in his life. He said to me, "If I had the power, I would have freed you now because I can tell that you are a good man." After two hours he was called away, and another guard took over the shift. This one was the complete opposite of the previous guard. He gave me such a hostile look as he entered that it was perfectly clear he hated the sight of me. I said hello, but he ignored me. I continued reading my Bible.

A policeman entered the room with some forms for me to sign. I took the pen and scribbled my name on them, barely looking at the papers.

"You should have read them before you signed," the policeman told me, sternly.

"What difference does it make whether I read them or not?" I asked. "It won't change your mind about taking me back, will it?"

"We are not taking you home after all. The escort vehicles have been recalled."

I peered out of the window, and the cars that were meant to drive me to the airport had indeed disappeared. I could not believe my eyes. Completely overwhelmed with happiness at this sudden deliverance, my eyes welled up, and I began to cry. I realized what God had meant when He showed me that passage in Romans. He would never let me be ashamed again. My life would no longer be spent as an addict and a prisoner, bringing shame to my family. Instead I would do something to make them proud of me and give glory to God.

Chapter Thirteen

ALL THINGS ARE NEW

Once more I was a free man, but I was determined that this freedom would be forever. I was fiercely determined never to go back to the living grave that is the prison—never again to be a prisoner for as long as I live. I am grateful that I got another chance to make the right choice. Everybody has a choice in life of what path to follow. I repeatedly chose the wrong path and repeatedly made the same mistakes through my own greed and foolishness. Fortunately, it's never too late to make things right, and God showed me that in spite of all the bad and shameful things I had done, it was still possible to turn my life around and make the right choice. Instead of being trapped inside a prison as a felon, from now on, I would voluntarily enter the gates of the prison to bring my story to all those who were willing to listen—in the hope that they too would choose to make things right with themselves and with God.

Armed with this new determination and purpose, I took a flight from Sardinia to Rome and lodged in a hotel for a few nights. While in prison, I had done several odd jobs ranging from washing dishes to grazing cows in the prison fields—jobs I never thought I would do in my lifetime.

As soon as I checked into the hotel, I began to call my old friends at Padua to inform them of my release. One of them asked me how I was doing in Nigeria, as they already heard that I had been deported. As a matter of fact, he told me that somebody said he had seen me in Lagos the week before. He was speechless when I told him I was still in Italy. He said, "Solution, how did you do it?" To which I told him simply that it was God who miraculously set me free. Such is the awesome power of God; He is more than able to set the captives free, no matter the type of captivity—physical or spiritual.

And so I walked the streets of Rome again, but this time as a changed man. With my newfound freedom came the nagging worry of what to do next with my life. In addition to this was the extra burden of figuring out how to survive: my small savings was running out. I had to think of ways of making money fast, but unlike all the other times, drug peddling was no longer an option.

I knew I could not stay in the hotel for long. I had no idea where to go as most of my friends were either drug addicts, drug peddlers, or both. And as usual, I had nothing to go back to—no house, no car, no clothes, and no family. In fact, I had lost everything I had before my arrest. Faced with homelessnesss, I resisted the impulse to go to my "friends." Going to them would have meant going back to my former life. I killed time by visiting Christian bookshops in Rome. On one of these shops, CLC, I saw a flyer posted that advertised Dr. David Wilkerson's trip to Rome to minister to pastors. I made up my mind that I would be there as a pastor too. It was only my second day out of prison.

Finally, I decided to travel back to Padua where I used to live before my arrest and checked into yet another hotel with the belief that God would send help before my little savings ran out completely. And God did in the most unexpected way. It so happened that a few hours after I arrived in Padua, I found a local church called Sword of the Spirit Ministry (SOS), and I began to work for God. I became a very active church worker—helping out with church activities, inviting people to church, and serving as an interpreter in the church during services, using my fluent Italian to good advantage as most services were held in English language. The pastor of the church, Evangelist Evans, saw my commitment and determination to live right, helped me rent a room, and paid two months' rent for me.

During this time, my mission was to evangelize my former friends and draw them to Christ so they too could be free from a crime-filled life of addiction and wasted years. But while a few came willingly, the majority started avoiding me altogether. At first, some of my friends were very skeptical about my new life. Some even felt that I had finally lost it completely. Indeed, my new lifestyle sent tongues wagging: some people were very sure that I could not break free from drug addiction so easily. They felt that I would go back to a life of drugs and prison within months. But as days grew into weeks and weeks became months, they finally began to believe that perhaps I was truly a changed person. I think this in itself was a big demonstration of God's power to them because often I would hear people say, "If Solution can be free from drug addiction, anything is possible with God."

I think the one incident that truly convinced my old friends of the fact that I was a new person was when I forgave an old friend, Tony, who betrayed me. On the day of my arrest, I had given him five thousand euros to help me pay for a house he told me he had found close to the city where he lived. While in prison, I needed some money to pay my solicitor, so I sent Tony several telegrams asking him to send money to me, and to my parents. I asked him to do a few other things for me as well because I thought he was my friend, but he never responded to any of my letters or telegrams. I wrote to other friends, asking them to urge him to release my money to me, but he never complied. When I began to suspect that he had betrayed my trust, I started to send him letters threatening that I would make sure I got him killed unless I got that money back from him any day I got my release from prison, no matter when. Though he was not the only one who had some of my money before I got arrested, his betrayal pained me to the marrow because I trusted and believed he was my friend. I later realized he was a fake. I was determined to get rid of him, send him to an early grave, and go back to prison which had become my home anyway. He knew I was not kidding. But God had already arrested me in prison this time, and I came out a changed man.

On my release from prison, my friend refused to pick up any of my calls and avoided me completely. When he heard that I had been released from prison, he went into hiding because he knew that he had hurt me badly, and he thought that I was going to make him pay dearly for betraying my trust. I sent messages to him through some other common friends we had together, to tell him that his salvation had become more important to me than the money. At first he must have thought I wasn't serious about that, but when word spread that I was now actually fishing men, he showed up weeping. I was horrified when I saw how he had degenerated. I began to pray for him, preach to him, and eventually led him to Christ.

Gradually, I began to notice a positive shift in people's attitude toward me. My friends who were not into drugs and who during my prison days would only greet me from afar for fear of getting into trouble began to draw closer to me and even invited me to their homes. This was a risk they would clearly not have taken during my drug days for fear of a police raid on their homes. So it was during one such visit to a friend's house that I first felt the prompting of the Holy Spirit to minister healing.

I was sprawled on one of the beautiful sofas in Sunny's living room, eagerly awaiting the sumptuous African dish he was preparing for me when I noticed that he injected himself with a syringe full of some kind of liquid. Being an ex-junkie, I knew straightaway that it wasn't hard drugs. Upon my enquiry, he told me that he was diabetic and that he needed to have an insulin injection at a certain time of the day. When I asked him how long he would need to do that, he told me that it was going to be a continuous thing until his last day on this earth. I asked him, "Who said so?" When he told me that his doctor said so, I asked him if that was what God said to him. Then as I kept on ministering to him, his faith rose, and he went into his room, took out all the insulin and syringes in his house, and dumped them all inside the bin. With a determination in his eyes, he said, "Solution, I will never touch insulin again, and I will not die." This was around June 2002, and as I write this book, he has never touched insulin again. He is in perfect health and is now married with children. Ten years after, whenever, I go to preach at any church in Italy, he always comes to the church with his wife and children. God is *real*. He is Jehovah Rapha indeed!

This incident with Sunny further strengthened my faith in God and made me more determined than ever to continue to preach to my friends to abandon the life of crime. A few incidents come to my mind. One morning as I was coming down the stairs from one of the houses in Padua where I had gone to invite someone to church, I saw a few of my old friends using drugs—some sniffing cocaine, another injecting heroin, and others smoking crack cocaine on one of the staircases at Via Aneli, a very notorious drug place then. I had been arrested several times there in the past. The moment they saw me approach they said, "Here comes the 'evangelist'; let us see if he can resist drugs." They offered me drugs and were greatly stunned when I refused. One of the chaps, a Senegalese guy, said that if he watched me for a week and I didn't go back to drugs, he too would quit. I turned to the other guy with him, a Tunisian by the name of Hassan, another friend from the old days, and tried to persuade him to go to church with me. He bluntly refused and offered me about half a gram of crack. He too was surprised and impressed when I said no, and he gave me a fifty euro bill. I pleaded with him to give up drug use and start living a fruitful life, but he wouldn't listen. I warned him that a life of drugs would only lead him to destruction and an early grave. I left them and went to church while they continued with their drug use.

On my return from church three hours later, I learned that an argument broke out between Hassan and another Tunisian guy there on the staircase and a fight ensued. In the full view of people, as Hassan was having an upper hand in the fight, the other guy stabbed him in the stomach, and he bled to death before help could even arrive. Such was a typical consequence of life wasted on drugs. After witnessing the death of Hassan, my Sengalese friend needed no further urging to give up drugs. He would later confide in me that when he saw the huge transformation in my life, he began to nurture the tiniest hope and belief that perhaps it was possible for him also to live a drug-free life. At last I was becoming a positive influence in the lives of people.

At about this time, my two months' rent period was nearly at its end; I had to think of ways of making a living. The only option was to buy and sell things, and I chose to sell Christian books due to the fact that I wanted to make other people cultivate the habit of reading Christian literature. There was only one obstacle standing between me and my newfound profession—I had no money and no idea how to stock the Christian books. Again, help came unexpectedly. It came after my baptism by immersion. One of my friends, Edda Fogarolo, who also is an evangelist, had introduced me to a pastor friend of hers, Pastor Pietro Evangelista, who baptized me. Incidentally, Pastor Pietro Evangelista was and still is a Christian publisher. I spoke to him of my interest in selling Christian books instead of drugs. As I did not have money to buy the books, he agreed to give me various titles and Bibles on trust from their offices at Pescara, Italy. I would take these from houses to offices and to churches, and people bought from me. I suddenly became a Christian bookseller and no longer a drugs seller. I also made a few dollars to move my life forward until God made other ways of sustenance available. I was determined never to trade on drugs or live by any criminal ways again. Since then, God has been my Jehovah Jireh, my Provider, meeting me at every point of need.

My appetite for the things of God grew deeper by the day. I devoured many books written by great men and women of God. I read the Bible from cover to cover. I attended as many crusades and conferences as I could afford. Without much money, it was a big sacrifice to attend many of these events. Most times, I had to trek for long distances to attend them. During one such event, I met the late Dr. David Wilkerson who had been my hero from a distance. I admired him greatly because he was running a drug rehabilitation center (something I hope to be able to do in the near future). This conference for pastors and ministers of the Gospel was held in Rome, and even though I was not yet an ordained pastor, I felt a strong need to be at the event. It was the event I saw advertised in one of the Christian bookshops I visited in Rome. I managed to attend the event with no knowledge of where I was going to get the money for food or accommodation. Nevertheless, I attended the conference by faith. At the event, I met many pastors and evangelists from all over Italy, including a pastor from Bologna, who had given Frank Catania's book, *Appena in Tempo* to a prisoner who passed it on to me while I was in transit to Caltanissetta prison. He paid my hotel bill and took care of my food. How God arranges things! Indeed, the steps of a righteous man are ordered by God.

But I still had a deep yearning to do more for God. I wanted to devote my entire life to God's service. Following my conversion in prison, I had done a Bible course by correspondence and was keen to further this by going to a Bible school where I could study in English, since all the schools I found in Italy were conducted, naturally, in Italian. That was how I started thinking seriously of relocating to the United Kingdom. I had no clue how to achieve this; all I had was the trust and the belief that God would make it possible. Only one thing stood clear as crystal in my mind: a life of drug addiction was no longer an option— *never again.*

Epilogue

TRANSFORMATION

It is now over ten years since the day I turned away from drugs and decided to work for the good of the Lord. I am now married with children. I thank God that I am no longer the violent man I used to be toward women. That is another of His miracles. God has blessed me with a God-fearing woman who supports my ministry, and I am truly grateful to God for giving me another opportunity to be a good husband and father.

I run an organization in North London called SHADE (Saving Hands for Alcoholic and Drug End-Users) under the umbrella of the New Covenant Church, Edmonton. As you can see, God did, indeed, make it possible for me to relocate to England. It is now the base from which I carry on an outreach program for prisoners and drug addicts that I have built up over the past decade.

The aim of SHADE is not to judge anyone, but to help those who have been messed up by drugs, alcohol, and other forms of addiction to regain their dignity and self-confidence in order to fulfill their mission in this world—because life is not a dress rehearsal. SHADE follows up prisoners as well as ex-offenders irrespective of what crime they committed or where they hail from.

My mission is to offer every help I can to bring back freedom to those who have gotten entangled in the deceptions of drug addiction. In my experience, no broken life is beyond repair, and I want to share that with all those who are suffering the effects of a life of addiction. There is hope and healing to be found in God.

I have told my testimony in prisons all over the world. In the UK, where I now live with my family, I have been working to visit prisons across the country to use my story to inspire drug users to change their lives. In Milton Keynes, England, I met two addicts locked in a cycle of crime and drug abuse. After hearing the story of how God repaired my brokenness, they decided to get clean, and now they also use their experience to help others trapped in the same state of dependency and despondency.

I have also told my story in Italy. It was indeed a happy moment to go back as an evangelist, instead of a drug addict. While in Italy, I told my story in several churches and in the prisons. Many people—many of whom had known me—came out en masse to hear me speak about mending broken lives. Even one of the senior police officers, after seeing my picture on the advertising posters, couldn't help but attend one of the events just to be sure that I was the same person he used to lock up in prison. Once he was sure that I was indeed the same person, he was so happy that he drew the media attention to the event. Thus, my visit caused a huge media sensation and of course, a revival, as many people could not believe the huge transformation in my life.

In 2007, I travelled to Sao Paolo in Brazil. I visited several prisons to share my testimony and offer prayer support to prisoners. One lady I met was contemplating suicide because she felt so alone and unloved. She was in prison for killing both her husband and her boyfriend. When she heard my story, and the news that God still loved her regardless of her crimes, she broke down and wept. In turning to God that day, she found that she was filled with peace and the strength to carry on in spite of her incarceration.

By the time I had spent four weeks in the city, the Commissioner of Police noted that many of the prisoners were a lot calmer, and there were fewer suicides. In trusting their worries to God instead of heaping worry upon themselves, prisoners had found their depression lift and their anger subside. The Commissioner was so pleased with the work I had done that he presented me with a small plaque, commemorating my visit and the help that I had offered to the inmates of the city.

I once travelled to Cardiff, Wales, to give a talk at the large prison there. Upon hearing my testimony, over forty prisoners came forward to give their lives to God, allowing Him to fill them with the strength to turn away from drugs and crime. The chaplain of the prison was surprised at the number of people who had come forward. He told me that he had been chaplain in that particular jail for thirteen years, and in that time, he had never seen such a response from the inmates. He asked me what my secret was. I said that it was the testimony that did it. All I had to do was speak the truth, tell others of what happened to me, and God would use it to inspire change.

Such is the power of a relevant testimony. It is the power of words of hope coming from somebody who has been in the same dark and hopeless place as the people he is speaking to. Words of hope which show that you can change your life—and with God's help, you need never go back.

Lawrence Oji with Cherie Booth, wife of the former British Prime Minister, Tony Blair

Lawrence Oji with British Prime Minister, David Cameron

Lawrence with some volunteers at the second anniversary of SHADE (Saving Hands for Alcoholic and Drug End-users), January 2007

One of several car wrecks motivated by a voice telling Lawrence to commit suicide

APPENDIX

One of the guys I introduced to cocaine and heroin is Keji Hamilton, a former drug addict, rapist, and band boy of the late Afro-Beat King Fela Anikulapo Kuti. He is now an ordained pastor to the glory of God.

On May 22, 2010, in an interview titled, "My Kalakuta Diary 2," Keji told the *Nigerian Vanguard* newspaper how he got into drugs. See excerpts of interview below:

Interviewer: So how did you get into drugs?

Keji : One Sunday afternoon, one guy came to me, He said, "Young man, I like the way you play. You are good." I said, "Thank you." He said, "Do you know, young boys like you use something in America which enhances their performance." And I asked what it was. He said, "Cocaine and heroin." And I told him I had never heard of it and that I am not interested because I was okay with the weed.

The guy said, "Look at you, you are a coward," and I said, "What?" You know you do not call a young man a coward. So I said, "Let me have it." And he gave me 5 grams of coke and 5 grams of heroin.

The guy is a drug trafficker. His name is Solution, but he is now a pastor in London. He taught me how to cook the cocaine and ways to consume drugs that night and left.

Ha, I didn't sleep that night. I took the first heat, and I went on stage. I was crazy and even somersaulted on stage (laughing). I said, ah! This thing *na gbangba, na helele*. I waited for the show to end and went back, locked myself in, and took the thing till next day. I was wide awake.

This guy supplied me the stuff for three weeks and disappeared. And that was it…that was how I got hooked to hard drugs, until I gave my life to Christ on the 7th of May 1994. Seventh of this May will be 16 years since I last touched drugs.

(Taken from the *Nigerian Vanguard*, http://www.vanguardngr.com/2010/05/my-kalakuta-diary-2/.)

Final Word

SOLUTION MINISTRIES— CHANGING LIVES...ONE AT A TIME!

Thank you for reading my story—*From Prison to Pulpit.* My earnest desire is that my testimony will help transform lives. I want you to know that with God all things are possible. There is no broken, battered, shattered, or scattered life that the Lord Jesus cannot turn around for the better.

Hence, it is my desire that you recommend this book to people and recommend people to us. Let this compelling account inspire you to pray for and reach out to all those you see imprisoned, either physically or spiritually, until they walk into the freedom which only the knowledge of and fellowship with Christ provides. In the words of Graham Dodd, "I think that God would like to see empty prisons."

If you would like to receive salvation, pray this prayer:

Father, in the name of Jesus, I come before You right now. I acknowledge that I am a sinner and I repent of every sin. Forgive my sins, O Lord, and cleanse me with the blood of Jesus.

I reject you, satan, and all that you represent.
Lord Jesus, come into my heart,
and make me a child of God.
Write my name in the book of life.
Thank You, Lord, for saving me,
in Jesus' name, amen.

Please get in touch with us if you need prayer, counseling, or if you would like to partner with Solution Ministries.

ABOUT THE AUTHOR

Lawrence Chukwugekwuihegeme Oji is a minister with the New Covenant Church in London, where he is coordinator of SHADE (Saving Hands for Alcoholic and Drug End-Users), a community project of his local church in Edmonton. Popularly known as "Solution," Oji has spoken at prisons in the United Kingdom, Brazil, Italy, and Nigeria and finds that his ministry as evangelist and pastor finds its fullest expression as he inspires others with his unbelievable story: a broken life once thought beyond the grave but now miraculously recovered and renewed. He is married to Stella-Maris, and they are blessed with three children.

CONTACT INFORMATION

Pastor Lawrence "Solution" Oji
Solution Ministries, London, UK

Email: solutionministries2001@yahoo.com

Youtube:www.youtube.com/solutionministriestv

www.facebook.com/lawrence.oji.9

Twitter: @solutionoji

Additional copies of this book and other book
titles from EVANGELISTA MEDIA™
and DESTINY IMAGE™ EUROPE
are available at your local bookstore.

We are adding new titles every month!

To view our complete catalog online, visit us at:
www.evangelistamedia.com

Follow us on Facebook
(facebook.com/EvangelistaMedia)
and Twitter (twitter.com/EM_worldwide)

Send a request for a catalog to:

Via Maiella, 1
66020 San Giovanni Teatino (Ch), ITALY
Tel. +39 085 959806 • Fax +39 085 9090113
info@evangelistamedia.com

"Changing the World, One Book at a Time"

Are you an author?
Do you have a "today" God-given message?

CONTACT US

We will be happy to review your manuscript
for the possibility of publication:

publisher@evangelistamedia.com
http://www.evangelistamedia.com/pages/AuthorsAppForm.htm